Navigating Insanity

One Man, One Mind, a Whole World of Questions

Larry Bentley

authorHOUSE®

AuthorHouse™
1663 Liberty Drive
Bloomington, IN 47403
www.authorhouse.com
Phone: 1-800-839-8640

First published by AuthorHouse 4/20/2011

ISBN: 978-1-4567-6084-7 (e)
ISBN: 978-1-4567-6085-4 (dj)
ISBN: 978-1-4567-6087-8 (sc)

Library of Congress Control Number: 2011906249

Printed in the United States of America

Table of Contents

Forward

By: Troy Martin

After knowing Larry for about 10 years now, we've had the time to discuss many topics and make a few memories. Larry is not always right nor is he always wrong but his opinions and advice come from the heart. When he first told me about this book, it didn't surprise me at all, he is an ambitious and intelligent person. Read these words as if you are talking to him and looking him in the eye.

    I'm proud of what he has done here and I'll bet you and your friends talk about some of the topics mentioned after having read this book. Serious or funny, a good conversation is all it takes to know your fellow man, so enjoy these pages. If they make you laugh, scream or both… mission accomplished.

Troy Martin

Preface

My Motto:
"Success is measured by how high one bounces after they have hit bottom."
Gen. George S. Patten

My name is Larry Bentley. I was born in a small town in Iowa called Bluffton. On the 3rd of March 1968 I was born to Merlin and Alice Bentley and grew up on the family farm. With my brother and sister we lived a relatively normal childhood. I played and dreamed the same as any child did, but would start at an early age to question the status quo. I questioned politics when my mother's cousin was killed in Vietnam, and I questioned religion as I watched my grandparents die and then as a teenager I watched my friends start to die off.

I had little time for school. Not because I thought education was wrong, but because I can't agree with conformity, and I strongly disagree with the system, and I will discuss those views in detail later. By the age of sixteen I was a strong willed and brash young man with a disillusioned view of the world. I could not wait to fix the world nor was I willing to do so the way everyone thought was correct.

At the age of seventeen I joined the US Army and went into the Infantry. I served proudly for four years and was taught many things that would follow me through the years. In the military I learned the meaning of words like sacrifice, loyalty, duty, honor, and many more. I also learned the meaning of true friendship. With great confusion I also come to understand that all positive things are not necessarily good, and in contrast all negative are not bad. In other words; sometimes the right thing to do is the most terrible and sometimes the wrong thing seems to just have to be.

After the Army I went on to learn a whole new set of words such as excess. Excess would come to symbolize the next six years. Extreme alcohol usage along with drugs and sex were all accepted normal behavior for a musician. I was a self taught guitar player and would become the lead guitarist for a band called Raging Angel. Our drummer would one day be my wife and our days were filled with excitement, chaos, and fear. Here too I come to understand business. After all, music is an industry all its own. I learned about marketing, sales, finance, and most importantly I learned that to succeed I needed to live breath and die "music" if necessary. All was for the band. One doesn't succeed because they want; one only succeeds through sacrifice, commitment, and dedication to the goal, <u>no matter what</u>. This worked for the most part. Six years later we had three albums that no one ever heard. We wrote and copyrighted more than one hundred and twenty songs. Fear of public speaking, simply no longer mattered, self confidence had taken hold for ever and it would never be a problem again.

Now by the age of twenty seven, I was married and had already had a seaming wondrous life. Bigger and grander than most or at least that was how it felt. I then realized that the one thing that I had not tried was the normal everyday life of the average person. The person that got up, went to work, came home, ate supper, and then went to bed, just to do it all over again the next day. That is not to say that this life needs to be boring. Quite the opposite is the reality of it. I started a factory job at a nationally recognized manufacturing company. While there I learned to read blue prints, build trailers, weld, and think on my feet in a productive manner: This led me to the other jobs that I did while there. I was a supervisor, quality control, and I worked in customer service. I then started to understand the inner workings of business.

After many years of working for this company I went on to participate in the forming of two other businesses. The first one was just my wife and me. We attempted to open a small auto parts store in Cresco Iowa. Our business plan was solid yet as any CEO would tell you, it all comes down to money in the end, and that is where we failed. Failure is but another lesson for all of us to learn. This experience taught me some valuable lessons about the sometimes uglier side of business.

Money is business. When I entered into my second venture, it was as a production consultant. I worked for free under the premise that if the company was successful, I would be rewarded. That was another important lesson. It was my job to help design and improve the production process. This business was very successful for about the first year and for reasons unknown to me, the owner and financier of the company started to get cold feet and suddenly wanted out. After desperately trying to raise the funds to buy the company the owner finally locked the doors and walked away. Again money had trumped the aspirations of one who had vowed to change the world, by whatever means necessary.

It was during these last years when time started to catch up with us. My wife got sick and was diagnosed with COPD (Chronic Obstructive Pulmonary Disease) and with time her medication would cause her to have problems with her eyes and bones. I have systematically watched as my wife began to slowly fall apart. I started to suffer from depression and anxiety and as my alcohol bill increased, my life and my house started to fall apart as well. My adventures with alcohol eventually caused me to injure myself. One night during a party I tripped and fell over a lawn chair and dislocated my shoulder. The fall caused a type III A/C separation of the right shoulder which led to the forfeiture of my job.

From there I decided to do exactly what I have always done. When faced with defeat one only needs to face into the wind and fight. Feeling sorry for one self and telling everyone that there's nothing I can do only makes things worse. If all you want to do is lie down and die; that is exactly what will happen. Stand and fight you may have a chance, and even if you don't win your no worse off then you started. Gen. Patten once said; *"Success is measured by how far one bounces after hitting bottom."* (Gen. Patton) So the way I decided to fight back was to go back to school. I started by getting my GED and started college. I have an AA degree in Business and one in Accounting and am presently working on my BA in Business Law with a minor in Human Resources.

With all this said, I will now turn my attention to the why rather than who. I am writing this for some fairly simple reasons. The simplest answer is the most obvious and most basic: money. Or at least I hope I can sell a few of these. Another reason is the idea that I have never done it before, and I certainly have never let that stop me before. I see this as a challenge of will. Everything in life can be broken down to the concept of will. Who has the will to succeed? Courage and will drive the world. The people that succeed need to have the courage to try and clearly they need the will to survive.

So why read my book? I am clearly not an expert, rich or famous. What I am is a person that has seen many different facets of life. I have seen the good and the evil in mankind, made promises I couldn't keep, and fought bleed and struggled to keep mankind in my heart and to not relegate them to the reaches of despair and disillusion.

This book is a descriptive metaphor of my opinions and thoughts. I will address many complex and controversial subjects including; warfare, abortion, religion, and many more. These are the thoughts and opinions of an average guy with deep feelings about many things. I wish only to share my views to support those who feel similar or have had similar experiences. I wish also to uplift those who have fallen and are wondering if or when their rebound will start. I will discuss ways to help when all seems lost. Parts will hopefully be funny, others will be very serious. All will be just my point of view.

I dive into many different subjects because as I started, I found it increasing difficult to explain the subject, without explaining how I come to that conclusion. For example: Can anyone really hope to explain way war happens if we don't look at ethics, morals, religion, and politics? Equally so: Can anyone really understand some other person's reasons for their beliefs on religion or politics if they don't understand where they are coming from? I do hope to write other books in the future, and I hope to focus on history, but for now this may be a good chance for you the reader, as well as for I to get to know me a little better.

To have the courage to question starts with the ability to understand those you disagree with. I hope to illustrate and explain some of these points of view. So even for those who would disagree with me I will try to put into words the thoughts and feelings of someone who does not wish to change your mind, just explain my opinion.

In closing, I want to encourage you the reader to just keep an open mind, and always have the strength and the will to question. As I stated I have no wish to insult or to deprive anyone of their beliefs. Just ask yourself the questions I bring forward and try to understand the world from another point of view.

The name of the book refers to the way I feel sometimes when I get deep into thought about some of the subjects that I will discuss in this book. I feel sometimes as if I am truly "Navigating Insanity" when I try to analyze different aspects of the human condition. We can endlessly choose understanding, and in turn offer considerations, and compassion for others, but fail to be able to agree about some relatively basic questions of our time seriously amazes me. I realize that we can't all agree all the time, but we certainly should be able to understand and even appreciate others point of view. Furthermore: the very idea of trying to write a book makes me feel that maybe I have lost it, at least a little. I close by saying that while you are trying to navigate the insanity, at least you won't feel alone. There are many opinions in the world, and you have to remember that your opinions are just as valid as anyone else's.

Dedicated to:
My wife Dena for her love and patience.
My extended family Chad and Sandy and Ron and
Carol for their guidance and friendship.
My friends Trevor, Troy, Jen, Rob, Dawn, Spry, Willie, Tim, Kim,
and Shannon for their support and sacrifices that they have all made.
I thank you all.

Special thanks to:
My Uncle Junior Klegseth for proving that if
you want it bad enough you will get it.
And
To My Grandpa Lyle F. Bentley; I wish you could be here.
And
To my Niece Allison; the closest thing I ever had to a daughter.
I love you all.

For all of you that are not mentioned:
I didn't forget you and never will: You all know who you are.

Chapter I

Ethics and Morals

To deny even one person a right, is an atrocity upon mankind.
We must remember that some of the worst atrocities have been
committed by those who would call themselves righteous.
We all need to remember that to disagree with someone
or something does not make it wrong.

Ethics and morals are the backbone of our society, yet we allow the rich and famous to show us how we should act. In the 80's it was almost fashionable to be the drug user that makes a commercial were they state "just say no." No one believed this crap, so why waste time doing it. It was done to satisfy the believers. There are millions of people out there that think that if a movie star says it; it must be true and if a sports star uses it; it must be the best. We all know that just because we buy the same brand of clubs as Tiger Woods, it won't make us better golfers.

So why is it when a movie star or sports star endorses a controversial subject by choosing one side or the other, people think we are all going to jump on board and follow like children. When I read or hear about some wonderfully rich and famous idiot trying to tell everyone how they should live, I just pretend they don't exist. A good example of this is Global Warming. It is my honest opinion that the Earth will continue to warm and if we are able to fix it; it will happen with or without Al Gore. I may not be rich, a great golfer, famous, or even good looking, but I will say that I still consider myself a better person and better man then Tiger Woods. At least I have never cheated on my wife. Being rich and famous doesn't make it OK. When I hear some of these guys talking about how the average person wouldn't understand what it's like. I just want to scream.

I mean look: these "important" rich people don't understand anything about real life yet they love to try to show us how we should live: Like I need Sarah Palin telling my wife and I whether or not we should have an abortion. I wouldn't take her advice on how to act like an idiot, [which she is good at] so why would I listen to her opinion or advice on something as important as our future?

As long as we are on the subject of abortion, I would like to explain my position on the subject. Freedom of choice is a simple and fundamental part of being human. Animals rely on instinct to guide their decisions; people have the ability to reason. What good is reason, if someone has already decided for you the "right" choice? Freedom of choice is just that. "The freedom": to choose to have a child, put it up for adoption, or have an abortion. No one is trying to force anyone to do anything. People like Sarah Palin would if we let them take those choices away, because they believe their way is the only way. It is my belief that people like that are just terrified of giving people choices or rights. It's as if they think the Constitution should read: Freedom of religion "as long as it's an excepted religion" or maybe it should say that we have the freedom of speech as long as it don't offend anyone.

I have heard the argument that abortion is killing. The myriad of opinions on which these arguments are based are pure conjecture. Your overzealous religious types believe life starts at conception, yet I have never read anywhere in the bible that says that. It's as if they called God up just to get his opinion on the matter. The reality is they don't know so just to be sure we should all be strapped down with unwanted children, who can grow up in homes that are unprepared and ill-equipped to raise children.

Their belief that abstinence should be the only birth control and anyone that gets pregnant because of an accident should have to pay for this mistake for the rest of their lives. Strangely enough these are same people that think our legal system is too harsh when it comes to teenagers being treated as adults. A teenager gets high and kills someone they do twenty years or so. Teenager gets pregnant they are supposed to pay for it forever. What makes it worse are the children that these proponents think they are saving will end up paying for it as well. Being born into a welfare system with a single parent household, just because someone else has a guilty conscience is a poor excuse for humanity.

I have several friends that have and are raising children in single parent households and in some of those cases I would say they do a better job than the two parent version. All would tell you that they love their kids and would do anything for them. Well of course they would. Anyone with kids would say the same and therefore cannot imagine life any other way. However most would say that if their daughter got pregnant that they would wish for an abortion, because if they could help them avoid the hardships they went through they would. Like a friend of mine said; "I wouldn't trade my kids for anything, but I would not wish that type of life on anyone. I want my children to go to college, have fun, fall in love, and when the time is right, then have kids, but only when they choose."

I am not saying that single parents are dire; in truth I don't care if there are one or ten parents. It doesn't make any difference if they can't care for the child or don't want the child. Why is having a choice such an appalling thing, especially if that alternative has no consequences for the people trying to pass the law. When my wife and I decided to have an abortion, how did it harm any of these people that think it should be against the law. I am not trying to convince anyone to get an abortion; therefore I get tired of people telling me what I should do. Maybe we need to learn to live our life and let others live theirs.

Maybe that child that was aborted would have grown up to be president, or find a cure for cancer. I say: maybe that kid might grow up to be someone like Jeffery Dommer or some other serial killer or maybe the next Adolf Hitler. If we are going to spar over what if, let's make sure we address all the possibilities, and not just the ones we like. The fact is we will never know either way. We could all argue about how the world would be if Hitler's mother would have aborted him, but that isn't what happened, so that position is senseless. These are all just perfect examples of how people think that other people should all believe the same as they do.

Another concept to think about is this. The issue of same-sex marriage has become a dividing point for many people. I find it fascinating to think we live in a world where we fight and fight for equality and at the same time try to segregate and demonize people for their beliefs. If I were to refuse to hire someone for being gay, I would be in a lot of trouble. What would happen if someone suggested that gays and lesbians should not be able to vote? I would hope that we all know the answer to that. So if gays and lesbians have the same rights as anyone else when it comes to the law, voting, human rights, or any other right that we all have, why don't they have the right to marry? The law says that sexual orientation is protected by law and a person cannot be discriminated against because of it, unless religion says otherwise or our state disagrees. I will explain my views on religion later in the book.

As for my personal thought on the subject, I definitely disagree with same-sex marriage and don't personally like homosexual behavior. That is simply an opinion. I do, however believe that people have rights, even people who practice lifestyles I don't care for. I do have acquaintances that are gay and I don't treat them different than anyone else. For me it is the same as hanging out with a Christian or someone Jewish. I don't agree with their religious views. That doesn't make them bad people and should never take away their rights for happiness and the ability to fulfill their dreams just like anyone else.

What possible problems come from allowing same-sex marriage? The Earth could stop producing offspring? Maybe lions will fall in love with deer and pandemonium will ensue? Maybe people would be forced to accept that other people may believe differently. Isn't that quite the quandary? The bible says that God destroyed Sodom and Gomorra because of their evil ways. The word sodomy comes from this story. Of course that only matters if you believe in the bible and the stories it tells. If same-sex marriage is legalized it would symbolize that people have turned away from the word of God. For the true believer this is the end of everything. The only thing that it is the end of is the church's power to influence human rights and impose their will on others.

For the naturalist the act of having sex with one's own sex is against nature. Well I grew up on a farm and I have seen many examples of cattle, dogs, horses, and sheep mounting each other as a show of dominance and even just for fun. Before anyone gets upset, I am not suggesting that just because animals do it that must make it OK. I will make many references to animals in my thoughts, and for those who are offended by these comparisons I would show my dogs as example. They are loyal, courageous, loving; clearly things we would never want to emulate. Naturalists concern themselves with many things such as same-sex marriage, because it is an affront to Mother Nature. Mankind is an affront to Mother Nature. We pollute, destroy, burn, and then try to manipulate everything around us. I love how naturalists will argue about Mother Nature, and will do so while talking on their cell phone. If Mother Nature wanted us to have cell phones why did she wait 4.5 billion years to let us have them?

Has anyone ever noticed that it is virtually imposable to have a conversation without the subject of racism or sexism coming up? I am well aware that both exist, but that doesn't mean that just because I didn't want Hillary Clinton to win the presidency, that didn't have anything to do with her being a woman. I don't know how many times I had to defend my position on that subject. As a white male citizen I simply had no chance of being right. Anyone that didn't vote for Clinton was sexist and anyone who didn't vote for Obama was racist. This became even more ridiculous when my wife got into an argument after saying she would not vote for Clinton, and a whole group of women were all fired up over the fact that it was our first real chance to elect a woman. I was under the impression that we should vote for the person that we believed could do the best job, not what sex or race they are.

Maybe racism will never go away until people stop using it to justify everything. When a white cop shoots a black man he is a racist. If a black cop shoots a white man it is because the man left him no choice. Look at the redundancy stupidity of the phrase "hate crime". It's as if you murder someone "that is bad," but if you murder someone and you hate them as well "then you are really in trouble." What's next? Maybe we should have a "love crime" for people who loved their victims. As a white male, if I do anything other than bring people of color and women to the top of the class so to speak, I am a racist, sexist pig.

Recently I was watching a program on modern racial trends on CNN. The show depicted children being shown cartoon characters of other children of different colors. They were asked to determine which child in the picture was the smart child, or the good child, both of which are unanswerable by any honest adult. These tests revealed with no surprise that the children; "both white and black" indicated that the white children were the preferred race.

First thing is the fact that there is no right answer to the question, in fact there is no answer at all. Nobody can determine intelligence, or behavior based on looks alone, much less the color of their skin. The kids are just responding to the question the way they think is expected of them. They believe that will make the person asking the question happy. This test is so easily biased that it shouldn't be considered valid at all.

Then there was the subject of "self segregation." (Study conducted by CNN and Dr. Margret Spencer) Apparently we segregate ourselves from people of different color, religion, or sex without even being aware of it. It seems to me that we are talking about some fundamental stupidity. I am a white male; I like heavy metal music, who is married with no kids. I don't spend a lot of time with people who like country music, nor have kids. This isn't because I am prejudice against people that have kids, I just happen to enjoy my time with my friends when the kids aren't around, or until they're old enough to be part of the conversation. Just because I don't hang out at country bars, or go to rap concerts, doesn't mean that I have a problem with the people that do. It means that we have different tastes. Pretty soon we will be judged based on what color cloths we buy. Maybe the fact that I prefer blue-jeans proves that I'm prejudice.

So let's look at self segregation from a different point of view. We exclude ourselves from other groups of people every day. Christians hang out with other Christians, white collar with white collar, and so too does most of the world. The psychology Professor that came up with this idea probably hangs out and spends time with other medical professionals, people of academia, or like minded people. I highly doubt she spends much time at a back yard barbecue with a group of blue collar workers. Does that in turn make her prejudice?

I feel that the problem with this theory is that there is no theory. This psychologist simply succeeded in making an observation that any five year old child could make. I conducted this experiment myself with my niece and a couple of her friends as the core group. We went to a park where I would point out different groups of kids. I would ask if they were kids that they liked, or played with, or got along with. They didn't like the first group of boys, because they were the jocks; "all they care about is sports" was the girl's immediate response. The second set of guys; were just "weird". They third group was a group of young girls, and the only reason they didn't like them was because they were only 8th graders. Last there was a group slightly older than them and their reaction to them was; "they're cheerleaders, they think they can do whatever they want."

In every case the reason for their dislike was completely superficial, based on simple similarities or differences. There was no mention of anything that had transpired to harm them or cause them to dislike the others just that they were different and liked different things. It is what it is, and I feel that we have to stop trying to find demons behind every door.

We can't create equality by suppressing the rights of one over another, no matter what color or sex or religion. I have many friends of color as well as the opposite sex, and I can honestly say I am not sexist or racist, end of story. Here's another example. When a female friend of mine needed her brakes changed on her car I offered to change them for her. Her immediate reaction was: "Can't the poor old city girl handle it?" I told her; "Change them yourself." Her boyfriend and good friend of mine finally convinced her that I was just trying to be nice and save her some money by doing it ourselves instead of taking it to a garage. Why do things have to be so problematical and why do people always think there is a hidden agenda.

Just as in the case with Hillary Clinton, why can't a person offer to help or make a decision based on their intellect and values? When I offer to help a male friend they don't think that I assume they can't do it, I am just trying to help. In the example with Hillary; I just didn't feel that she was the person for the job and it had nothing to do with the fact she was a woman. It sometimes seems as if the whole country has been brainwashed to think if they don't win, it must be because of their sex, religion, color, or one of the many others.

It appears to me that we, (the race of man) are so consumed with the need to be different. Yet when we achieve it, we categorize it, and then stereotype its characteristic so as to deprive it of its uniqueness. By doing so all resemblance of that in which we so desperately wish is lost. I would say that yes I am an individual. Let's look at that for a minute. I am a: male, Caucasian, forty two years old, married, no kids, ex-military, and on and on. All of these put me nicely into someone's idea of a category. This is true for everyone. We just can't acknowledge the reality that we are dissimilar and always have been. This is so abundantly true with regards to racism and sexism, but I believe more so with the battle of the sexes.

The way I see it, we need to look past the racism/sexism perspective. The only way we will ever achieve equality will be to stop expecting special treatment. I know this sounds counterproductive, but if it even appears as if one class or another is getting an advantage, the equality will not be realized. Promoting someone just because they are female or a person of color is just as wrong as promoting a person because they are male.

Through Affirmative Action we have forced companies to do just that. How can a woman ever hope to be treated equal if everyone thinks the only reason she got her position is because of some law or policy.

This is true in the immigration issue as well. These people want to be treated as equal American citizens, but they don't have to do what every other citizen has had to do. Yes, my entire family was immigrants at one time. Every one of them came through Ellis Island and applied for citizenship, paid their taxes, and obeyed the laws. The undocumented or illegal immigrant problem is as simple as this. They want equality without living up to equal standards and requirements.

I say simply, let's just allow all of them to become citizens. We can start by making them pay all the back taxes that they would have paid for the duration of time they have been here. This is of course they pass a background check, a drug test, and can speak English. These are all the same requirements that any other immigrant must meet. So let's start treating them as equals. In other words, throw out the ones that will not comply with those rules. I believe being American to be a privilege, not a right. I am not against immigration or equal rights for anyone. I just believe those rights be earned the same as they are for anyone else.

This brings me to the next subject that gets on my nerves at times. That is how ethics finds its way into so many everyday arguments. At times it appears to me that even the shear idea of death is somehow unethical. I have heard things such as the drinking age, smoking, cosmetic surgery, and the unemployment rate referred to as ethical issues. When did we become so blind? For example: When Hurricane Katrina hit New Orleans it was said that if it would have hit a city with mostly white people it would have been evacuated more quickly and the dikes would have been built better. It almost sounded to me as if this person was accusing the government and even Mother Nature being racist. The government dropped the ball and the hurricane was a catastrophe, but I can say with confidence that racism had nothing to do with it.

Death itself is a subject that can compel people to all sorts of emotional and at times irrational thoughts and behaviors. After all death is something that all people face and cannot be avoided. Yet we endlessly search for ways to stave off the inevitable. Plastic surgery makes us look younger and medicine has made it possible to live longer, but still the shadow of death lingers and hangs over us like a dark cloud in the distance.

I have many times wondered why people fear death so absolutely. A religious person has a wondrous place awaiting them. The naturalist understands the circle of life. Even the pessimist is capable of realizing it doesn't matter because we are all going to die at some point regardless of our beliefs. So where does the fear originate. Simply I think it comes from the oldest fear there is and that is the fear of the unknown. I'm not questioning anyone's convictions or beliefs. It has always seemed strange to me that if there is such a great place waiting for you? Why would you be afraid to go, is beyond me. There are dozens of wonderful places in the world, such as Disneyland, Yellowstone, or the Grand Canyon. I can honestly say that I am not afraid of these places and I am certainly not afraid to go. Maybe it's not the destination that scares people. Perhaps is the method of travel that frightens. After all, to get to Heaven, one must die.

So let's look at some of the things people are compelled to do in the name of preserving life. Some would try to force people to have children that are both unwanted and if we look at the population: un-needed. We try to regulate what people can do to themselves. For example the smoking ban; who benefits if I quit smoking? Some would argue that my life would be improved and I would live longer. As to improving my life: It would only be improved if you believe that taking away a person's freedom of choice an improvement.

Many people seem to be psychic when it comes to people's health. I have been told countless times that smoking will kill me. Obviously I am being told this by someone that will die just as assuredly as I will. This is also presumptuous in that they knew how long I would live had I never smoked. I don't know anyone with that kind of personal relationship with god. The "facts" are all based on statistics and the law of averages, and still worse, people's opinions. Regardless of where the facts come from it seems to me that it's my life, let me live it and if it makes you feel better let me throw it away. The fact that I smoke does in no way affect your life or standard of living. Some would say that it raises health care costs.

OH money. Money runs it all. When people can't find any other way to win a disagreement it always comes back to money. In the smoking debate the argument is that smokers cost tax payers money. Never mind that smokers pay higher insurance premiums, taxes on the cigarettes, plus the higher out of pocket cash at the doctor. Let's not forget that cigarettes are not the only unhealthy activity that people have. People have countless hobbies and life styles that can lead to health problems and death. Things may include; obesity, drinking, drugs, and failure to obey traffic laws. All one has to do is read the warning labels on the things we purchase. Computers and televisions have been cited for causing epilepsy, cell phones for causing brain cancer, and car accidents maim and kill thousands yearly. If anyone were to suggest that we regulate or ban such things the world would probably fall into chaos.

Then there are the things man hasn't created. Disease for example is something we can't necessarily control and certainly didn't invent. So how do we deal with Mother Nature? We treat it, we prolong it, and we charge for it. Anything but cure it. Mankind has never cured a single disease yet we spend millions and millions each year to try to halt the path of nature. Critics would undoubtedly argue that it is simply unethical to allow people to die from disease, yet they find it perfectly OK to drive them into bankruptcy and poverty to pay for their treatment. Treatments that will not work or do anything other than prolong one's life for the purpose of keeping the money rolling in.

Think back to the last time you heard someone's death referred to as natural causes. If an eighty year old person dies of a heart attack; that to me is natural causes. Yet there will still be those who will say that he or she would have lived to be ninety if they didn't smoke or drink. People are just never satisfied. There are more than sixty thousand people in the U.S. over the age of one hundred and we still think we need to figure out how to prolong life.

We have even outlawed suicide. How ridicules can we get? I agree that suicide isn't something that I wish for anyone, but if someone has become so disgusted with life, who in the hell do you think you are to say that they can't end it if they so chose. Here again is just another example of control. The power to control those around us is what guides our principles and our laws. So many of our laws are designed to end human suffering, but there are some designed to prolong suffering. If a person has come to such a dark and desperate place as suicide, maybe they are the only ones that know what is best for them.

Now don't get me wrong, I have no desire to depart any earlier than anyone else, and as a soldier I faced that reality several times. I am just saying that dictating life to others is wrong. Dictating how one lives and what they should or shouldn't do, as well as dictating the how and when they can die is just utterly disgusting.

Where are the ethics in the conversation on overpopulation? The answer is: No one wants to talk about it. On one hand there is the group of people that don't believe there is or ever will be a problem. Then there are the people that think it will all be just fine because our wondrous brains and technology will come to save the day.

The ethical issues surrounding the right to procreate are both intense and passionate. Overpopulation is not just possible but it will happen eventually. According to some scientists, it will come sooner rather than later. Some estimates claim that the United States will top one billion by the end of the century and a colossal twenty billion in the world by the same time. It may be unlikely that some people would not consider this overpopulation, but what will the population be in another hundred years, or a hundred after that. At some point it will happen. Maybe we will address this problem the same as all other problems. We could just wait till it's too late.

What are some of the major problems? Well I don't wish to insult anyone's intelligence, but for the purpose of addressing all the angles; I will do just that. Address all the angles. First we need to look at food production. As population grows so does the need for food; so as our population doubles then triples you can do the math. That is of course assuming that we don't develop any bio-fuel or bio-energy, both would undoubtedly increase that number exponentially. Again as the number of people expands the need for housing will also increase; therefore decreasing the potential space for the growing of crops. With several million people dying every year in the world from starvation: How can we assume to feed the millions more who are to come?

Second thing we should think about is these people's additional needs. Needs including; health care, jobs, housing, space to dispose of their garbage, and places to bury the dead. Some of these things may not be so obvious, but I will discuss each in turn. Health care should be as obvious as the rest. However, I feel I should point out that when populations become compressed into increasingly smaller spaces, illness and disease are much harder to control and prevent.

Employment is a whole other matter. At the population rate of today, we need to create approximately one hundred thousand jobs each month. Picture having to create jobs for a quarter or even a half a million every month: Especially when we live in a culture that is continuously trying reduce labor costs. These two goals are at odds with each other, and as long as we breed at will, corporate America will always reap the benefits of an over populated work force.

Thus far I have pointed out the basic needs a culture must provide to sustain its society. Remove even one of the three the culture suffers and eventually dies. That however isn't the end. We still have to dispose of our garbage, consume the resources, bury our dead, and produce fresh water, and undoubtedly a few things I forgot. The last thing that needs to be addressed is crime and warfare. Both are common place in over populated countries. On the up side, both do reduce the population, but I would hope that there could be a better solution.

Now I am not a heartless bastard that supports mandatory abortions, or euthanasia of the sick or elderly, but there must be a way. Otherwise it is my opinion that our future is limited to decades; not centuries. I believe this is not just another one of those problems that we can just wait and hope technology somehow comes to the rescue.

Technology, fantastic technology, OH the wonderful magical: OH hell you get the idea. Technology is our new God, followed by money and his sidekick science and progress. Technology in my opinion has become part of the quandary rather than the solution. Ask yourself: When was the last time I saw an invention that was truly designed for the benefit of mankind? Before the critics can point out the obvious; I would say that all medical technology and pharmaceuticals are created for profit, nothing else. The point seems to be to produce anything people will buy and to produce things people need. The things we want are priced accordingly. Based on how bad someone wants it. For the things that people need, they get priced according to how bad people need them. The more we need something the higher and higher the price.

Pollution is an example of where technology has failed us. We can reduce pollution with several methods that all of us have at our disposal every day. However because of the inconvenience of that, we just wait and hope that the government will pass some law that will force technology to fix it all. On the other hand we will only stand for that if it does cost us anything and we don't have to change our habits.

The health care debate in Washington is another example of the futility of man. Out of fear of cost we would rather see people go without care. In my opinion anyone that is against health care are just as bad as the NAZIs of WWII, who felt that the sick and infirm should just go away for the benefit of the whole. The law of nature does dictate that the strong survive, does it not?

Let's look at the debate for a minute, because I have some concerns of my own. Why should I have to pay for other people's children with my taxes? Wait I already do. Why should I have to pay for other peoples stupid activities? Wait I already do. In fact I have spent twenty five years paying taxes for other people kids to go to school, and tax breaks because they exist. Then when it comes time for me to use some of those same benefits it was like asking someone to give up one of their kids. Sorry for being bitter but I can't help it.

All these different points of view to take in: provided you read far enough to get to this part. I would like to try to discuss some possible solutions to the differences. There are many fundamental things that I believe that we will never agree on, yet my friends and I are no exception. How do we manage to be friends even though we have greatly differing opinions? We listen, we talk, and we always do our best to understand the others point of view. I feel that success in any endeavor is accomplished by a group of people that don't agree. If we surround ourselves with people that agree with us, why not just talk to a mirror. To disagree doesn't make one wrong. To paraphrase what Patton once said: it proves that you are thinking.

I believe that the best way to start to solve some of our problems with racism, sexism or any of our dozens of other differences is simple acceptance. Accept the fact that people are different. Accept the fact that people will not always agree. Most importantly, we need to accept the fact that our way is not the only way. If we are to respect other people and cultures we need to accept the fact that they may disagree with us. Last: we need to accept the fact when we try to force people to see things differently, we no longer respect diversity. There is no diversity if we convince all people to think the same. In addition to all of that, we need to accept that the best thing for the whole may not be best for you or the few.

I feel very strongly that some of our other diversity problems can be solved by learning to not jump to conclusions. As I previously mentioned with the elections. At some point we need to accept that just because someone didn't vote for Clinton, that doesn't make them sexist. We simply must stop trying to find the hidden agenda in everything that people do.

Finally, I would like to say that when it comes to some of the problems that I discussed in this chapter: I don't have all the answers. I wish I did. With the examples of Global Warming and over population I know both will happen eventually. Time will tell if we are smart enough or courageous enough to overcome them.

Chapter 2

My Insight on Man

As long as we think that we are the masters of our domain,
it will be all the worse when the lease is up.
Sometimes it is in our darkest hours that we find the brightest light.
When bathed in light it is much harder to see the shadows.

What we are is a matter of academia. We are a mass of cells and DNA that make up a unique pattern that we call humans. Humans are a group of individuals that combined constitute the race of Homo-sapiens. The last of a long line of evolutionary changes that have led us to the modern world we live in. That is simple in the biological point of view. Who and what are we really? If we were outside observers of the progress of mankind, what would we conclude? Now the best thing to do is to address this from a purely non-racist, non-sexist, non-religious fashion. In my opinion, all of mankind is equal. For this portion of the book my opinions may offend, but I have seen some of the best and worst of man, and I must say the bad outweighs the good, by far.

In my opinion we are a race of people so hung up on ourselves that we can't see the reality around us. We all pretend to be appalled when we hear about all the starving children in Africa or other third world countries. Then we sit and complain about what our government is doing or not doing about it. The whole time stuffing our face with whatever it is that seemed important that day. When our government spends money on food, we complain about what it will cost us. Do we really think that by saying that we care about something or complaining

15

about it somehow proves that we a sympathetic group of people? Do you really think that talking about it helps anyone? We are in fact a group of selfish uncaring people that like to look good. If we talk and complain about it long enough somebody else will do something. Won't they?

Our egocentricity has no boundaries. Now just to be clear, I don't mean every last person is selfish and greedy, just that most people are. If you are one of the kind good hearted people in the world I am sorry if I offended you. As for the rest of you: well you get the idea. I say that our selfishness has no bounds because, look at what we will spend on a football game. Who the hell needs a 60 inch TV? We will spend hundreds and thousands of dollars on all kinds of junk. Now I have all kinds of junk as well as anyone else, I just don't think that people think enough about what that money could do for someone less fortunate. Then look at these people that make seven figures a year. They only think of themselves. The ones that do give large sums of money to charity make sure that they get their picture taken while handing someone the check. Are they doing it because they care or because it gives them good press?

We do the same thing with virtually every major problem in the world. Hell we don't even do anything about these problems in our own country. The tribes of Ethiopia have been killing each other for decades. They are trying to commit genocide. What do we do? Nothing! Other countries are and have committed several of these types of atrocities and we impose sanctions. We tell them that we will not sell you our valuable junk. They respond by buying that junk somewhere else. When Russia invaded Georgia the United States "strongly condemned the action. As if anyone cared. There is no strength in words without the action that could follow up those words. People don't obey the law because it's the law, they do it because if they don't there will be retribution. They say the pen is mightier than the sword. Show me one war, one crime prevented, or even one life ever saved by a pen. Can you cure cancer by writing about it? No, you need to aggressively treat it. Can you prevent a crime by writing a law? No, we must punish those who fail to obey. The law didn't save the life, but perhaps the possibility of retribution did. Write if you must, but make sure you have the will to carry through with the actions the pen writes and be prepared to act when the words fail.

Man's arrogance is another matter completely. We are not only smart enough to know that we have gained the capability to destroy the world, but we have the arrogance to be proud of it. The ability to destroy the world: What a joke. That has got to be arrogance and ignorance at its finest. I mean what are we talking about really? We are talking about the destruction of mankind and our civilization, not the world. The asteroid that impacted at Chicxulub on the Yucatan Peninsula in Mexico wiped out the dinosaurs was several hundreds of times more destructive than the entire Earths nuclear stockpile combined. The Earth survived. It caused widespread destruction and wiped out several species, but the Earth was not destroyed. That is also considered one of the small ones that have hit Earth. For example: the comet that hit Jupiter (Shoemaker/ Levy 9) created impact clouds larger than the earth.

We have come to the belief that the Earth is somehow here for us. We are one of the youngest species on Earth, yet without us the planet has no purpose. The reality here is that man doesn't have the ability to do anything. The ability to destroy the Earth is left to the Gods or the universe, or even Mother Nature, but not man. We can harm the planet; we can even cause the extinction of certain species of life, but I don't think we have achieved godhood yet. I do realize that many scientists would like to think of themselves as gods, but let's consider this in a fundamentally realistic way.

With the discussion of global warming, we see a perfect example of this arrogant view of ourselves. We have not only harnessed the power of the atom, put a man on the moon, and calculated Pi, but now we have figured out how to change the temperature of the planet and can apparently do it at will. That is what we think! Clearly we think we have caused global warming and by simply doing what morons like Al Gore believes we should do; it will all be fine. Now whether or not you believe in global warming isn't the point.

I do believe that the Earth is going through a change. If we caused it: It has taken between two and three hundred years of industrialization to create the problem. How do they think we are going to fix it in a decade or two? On the other hand; when was the last time you could trust the weather man to predict the weather tomorrow. Why would we believe these people when they are predicting thing decades and centuries from now?

As I already acknowledged, our superciliousness is second to none. Not only have we set into motion things that will devastate us all but if we do what we are told the contention is that we will survive and flourish. I see this arrogance when it comes to our place in the world we live in as well. We are the new comers to this world, yet we think that our opposable thumbs make us superior to all. How many times have you heard someone say: "It's just a dog!"? Well what do we really mean by that? What I think we mean is that because we can talk to each other and tell each other how great we are that makes us superior. Much the same way we did when we first encountered the Mayans of Central America. They didn't look, talk, dress, or believe the same things that we do as they were clearly less advanced than us.

The Mayans calculated calendars, and had a far better understanding of astronomy than we did at that point in time. There understanding of mathematics was superior, and even their skills in architecture were far beyond that of Europe, and still we thought we were better. In fact we believed we were so advanced that we felt compelled to advance all other cultures. We were so superior that for the cultures that refused this enlightenment, we pronounced death.

This superiority didn't stop with other peoples. Man feared the wolf. We then set out to destroy it. So what about the dog? Well anyone can tell you that the dog is just a descendant of the wolf. The wolf can trace its family origins back about 65 million years. That accounts for about 50 million years of evolution, during which the wolf survived and thrived before mans earliest ancestors existed.

We have this delusion that evolution favored man and gave us the right to rule over this earth. Why didn't the wolf evolve beyond their seemingly simple lives of hunting and mere survival? Maybe because they never needed to move beyond the boundaries that Mother Nature provided. They are born with the speed, strength, and even the knowledge that they would need for their entire lives. Our evolutionary path has not been that simple.

We evolved not out of our superior intellect, but out of the need to survive. Anthropologists have contemplated and argued for years about how and why we started to walk upright. They have done this because walking upright is not the best form of locomotion. Yet: Somehow we survived! Mostly threw accidental innovations and simple luck. This begs the question of; why did the wolf live for millions of years with apparently few changes in evolution? Maybe Mother Nature knows when she gets it right, and therefore no further changes are necessary. I think we are just an ongoing experiment. If there is a god he or she has got to be incredibly entertained watching us pretend to be in charge of our destinies.

This brings to mind the concept of intelligence. How do we measure intelligence? We assume that because we are capable of telling each other how smart we are that somehow proves our intellectual prowess. If we suddenly found ourselves stranded in the middle of nowhere, our ability to do math wouldn't help us survive. In fact our ability to do most things would be of little or no use to us at all. In Mother Nature's eyes we are very fragile and ill-equipped to deal with the day to day struggle for life. For example; one's knowledge of chemistry will do nothing for you if you don't know where to find the ingredients or minerals. This is why when the end of the world comes; our bankers and lawyers will be the first to go. They simply don't have any skills that matter. In my opinion we have forgotten and in some cases even forsaken the knowledge that really matters.

Ancient man used their intelligence for the betterment of the whole. We, today use our knowledge to better ourselves. There are very few things that we do for the benefit of the whole. We are only concerned with how things affect us as individuals. When we pass a law that doesn't affect us directly, we generally don't even care what it is. I am writing this while watching the disaster in Haiti. Thousands of people have the urge to come to the aid of people because they were unfortunate enough to live in the wrong place at the wrong time. Still we can't come to a comprehensive agreement about how to care for our own people. I see commercial after commercial about giving thirty cents a day to save the life of some child in Africa, but never hear a thing about saving those in our country that are going hungry.

Our intelligence has failed us in so many ways. We think that helping someone in another country helps us, but it doesn't. I would be willing to bet that you actually think that money goes to feed and cloths those children. If you are so smart, answer me this. Who pays for those commercials? Who pays for those camera operators, spokespeople, and plane tickets for them to go to these places? The bottom line is this. A not-for-profit organization is still allowed to make money, and pay their people well. If we can feed and clothe a child for thirty cents a day; how many kids could we feed and clothe with the money people spend on those commercials and the money that those executives make? While your thinking about that, ask yourself; how smart are we really.

So where does our intelligence fit in the grand scheme of things? It's my opinion that we have simply developed the ability to convince ourselves of our greatness. I have said that before, however I feel that it is worth saying again. I mean how many species can you think of that love nothing more than to sit around and discuss how great we are? After all is that not what we do? We measure, calculate, and regulate who and what we decide is intelligent. Those that do not fit so nicely into our categories are labeled, ridiculed, and regardless of equality laws are never quite the same as the rest of us. They are disabled, physically challenged, or some other polite word for inferior, yet inferior none the less. Just because we are polite about it doesn't mean that it changes anything. Now before anyone accuses me of being insensitive, let me remind you that I am married to a disabled person, and I see this every day.

The last insight on man that I feel compelled to discuss is man's never ending greed. We are the one and only species on the planet that can claim the sin of greed. More power, more money, more resources, more armies, more people, more, more, and the pattern will never end. Look at every problem we have in this world, and you will discover that greed is the root of all our problems. Starvation is the result of the people who have with no consideration for those that don't: As is the shortage of anything that is needed by the masses. We do not have the power to diminish what people need, but I feel or at least hope that we will someday have the power to alleviate, the over whelming need for wealth and possession. Only then can we find peace and show compassion for our fellow man. I love the fact that people will argue that they need money to survive, but when you ask them to give some to someone else they seem to think that the unfortunate party does not.

As I stated in the chapter on ethics; we are always waiting for someone else to take care of the problems of the world. During the recent earthquake in Haiti the American Football League and the National Football League donated 100 million dollars to the relief fund. That constitutes a small percentage of their merchandise sales for 2009, and barely scratches their bottom line if you include all of their income. They think by throwing big numbers around, we will all be so impressed that we will kiss their big fat behinds. Maybe if organizations such as the AFL/NFL were to donate 10 billion or some other amount that actually represents a portion of profits. This would show some measure of sacrifice.

Now I must say that I am glad that they gave something, but don't expect to impress me. On the other hand if you are doing it for the right reasons, you shouldn't be advertising what you donated anyway. Look at it this way: If all I could afford to donate was a hundred dollars that is what I would do. I would be proud of what I did whether or not it made the front page of the paper or not. Helping someone should never be reduced to a photo op.

So what is our place in the world? If we are not the masters of the planet what is our role in the grand scheme of things? I feel that we need to realize we are "part" of the whole, not the masters. Only man has the arrogance to assume that there needs to be someone in charge. We use the forests as if they were put here for our needs. We use the oil and natural gas as if it was meant for us alone. Even the animals around us were somehow placed here for us to do with as we choose. Now don't confuse me with some animal rights activist: I am a carnivore and I do eat meat. That however doesn't mean that I think animals are inferior or that we have the right to destroy or hunt them to extinction. If you kill an animal you better eat it or ware it. Any other reason is in my opinion murder.

When we try to involve ourselves in Mother Nature's business we just cause more problems. Maybe it is time we just accept the fact that we can't really change anything. During the Black Plague that ravaged Europe (1348-1350); the people killed the cats because some priest told them they were evil. We now know that it was the rats that carried the plague and if they would have just let Mother Nature do her job, the plague would have killed far less people.

Where I grew up farmers are always complaining about the deer population and how much of their crops they eat and destroy. I tell them maybe you shouldn't have killed all the coyotes and wolves. Then they tell me that they attack their cattle and live stock. Any zoologist could tell you that they only kill and eat the weak and diseased. By thinking they have saved their herds, they have in fact allowed disease to infect and kill more animals then the predators would have. Then they will say that we have vaccines for that. Well if you just left Mother Nature alone we wouldn't need such things and save that cost every year.

We try and try to regulate, dictate, and control our world. Time and time again we lose. We have dammed rivers, built levis to hold back the sea, and built earthquake proof buildings, yet time and again a simple snap of natures finger render all of our skill to dust. New Orleans was not destroyed by man, nor was it saved by man. As far as Mother Nature is concerned the wind blew and knocked over a few trees. She did however prove that if she wants us removed she has but to clap her hands and make us disappear. I don't think she cares for us much. She might however care about what we are doing to her planet.

I briefly mentioned some opinions about animals. I happen to love wolves and coyotes, and dogs in general. It is my absolute belief that they will be here long after we have gone. Make no mistake we too will go the way of the dinosaur. Someday, somehow, we will go! That is one thing that is without a doubt a fact, and there is absolutely nothing we can do to stop it. Why do I think they will be here after us? The same reason that most of nature will be here. They live in tune with the land, not off the land. We are a leech, a disease, and they have a symbiotic relationship with the world, we do not.

If we can't dominate the Earth and we can't dominate our fate, what is our purpose and to whom do we get to control. We can't control the planet so we try to control people. We can't control destiny so we try to control the animals and other parts of Mother Nature. We endlessly try to control everything, the populations of animals, viruses and bacteria, and even things like soil content. When we don't think that the soil is producing enough we add fertilizer. When a specific species starts to over populate according to our estimates we issue hunting licenses and have some of them killed. When a new disease comes along we attack it with every weapon at our disposal.

What about that disease? What if that virus allows us to find a cure for something else? Look at moldy cheese. We throw it away on sight and add chemicals to it so that it won't mold. Yet moldy cheese is where we found the ingredients for penicillin. What if we would have come up with a way to prevent the cheese from molding before we found the usefulness of the mold? Worse: what if the cure for some disease causes it to mutate into something else that is far worse than what we started with. We have been fighting the common flu virus for decades and maybe centuries. What we have started to realize is that every year it gets stronger and more virulent. Some even argue that by using live vaccines that we are unintentionally perpetuating the disease.

When we interfere with nature there is just no way that we can understand all of the possible consequences of the choices we make. In recent years there have been a continuous rise in cases of autism in kids and other disorders of this character. What if we discover that they have been all brought on by mans interference with nature. How many need suffer and die?

Let's discuss for a bit the role animals play in mans future, past, and present. Animals are our companions, guides, and inspiration for what we do and what we believe. That may seem to be a little bit of a stretch for some, but the fact is that many things from our sense of honor to our religious beliefs can in some ways be traced back to our animal brothers. For several ancient and not so ancient Native American tribes, this was more fact then legend. The wolf for example emulated our behaviors so much that the early Indians thought that they were the ancestors of the dead. Some would scoff at such an idea. If I were to describe a person to you that was: Loyal, courageous, faithful, and compassionate, you would probably think of him or her as a great person. These are not the traits of a person, but those of a wolf.

How can an animal be those things? They just do that because they don't know any better! When I look into the eyes of a wolf, I see all that we wish we could, or should be. The wolf mates for life. That is something that we are apparently incapable of doing. The wolf lives in a world in which the pack is all that matters. If one needs to sacrifice to ensure the survival of the whole than that is what happens. The alpha male is the leader, the beta male is his second, and finally there is the omega male (the fool). Their structure may seem harsh, but if you look at how it works, you too may be impressed.

Their loyalty is never compromised and I would never try to ascertain or assess their courage or resolve. Because of these they are the best example of a family, or government in the animal kingdom. That is at least my opinion. The early Americans modeled their tribes and family groups after what nature had given them. The pack lives in a family group with a hierarchal form of government. As I already stated the alpha is the top and his mate, the alpha female is the queen so to speak.

They mate for life; they hunt, protect, and die for the welfare of the pack. Nothing is above the pack. The alpha is in charge of the hunt, because he is the oldest and strongest. The beta is his right hand and is responsible for protection of the pack. He is surrogate mother, brother, and babysitter, because the young are the most important asset the pack has. Without the pups there is no pack. This is evident in the pecking order, when it comes to feeding. The alpha is first, to keep up his strength. The females are second, because they hold the future. The pups are next because they are the present. The rest of the pack follows according to the alpha's decree. The pack is loyal to their order to the end.

This has worked for them for 65 million years, and it worked for the Indians of the plains for hundreds, or thousands of years. We call it barbaric or primitive. What would you give for a leader that was loyal, genuine, courageous, and always looking out for our best interest? I wish our leaders could just understand such words. I doubt they would know what they mean without someone looking them up for them.

I don't believe that these are bad goals or virtues. Maybe I am just old fashioned or idealistic, but I think that traits such as loyalty, courage, and integrity are good human traits. Then add in self sacrifice for the betterment of the whole and compassion for the weak. OH; if we could only be so primitive?

When I analyze these types of behaviors I am left with a foul taste in my mouth. Man is so full of contempt and disgust with this world that we must think we are the masters and nothing else can match our malevolence for betrayal. They have no law, no constitution, and certainly no moral code, yet they live with higher honor and integrity then we do. If you are offended by this; you should be. An insignificant "animal" is better than we are.

The connection to man is clear. We observed these animals working together, and for the whole. It is not surprising that early man figured out that they may have an idea. The early natives saw them as equals, and as competition. Interestingly the early natives mimicked there hunting activities, and later even hunted side by side. Maybe it was a good thing that we whipped out the Native American cultures. How could we possibly live with a group of people that respected life? Including life of the Earth!

This respect for life didn't end with the wolf. Chief Crazy Horse was once quoted as saying: *"The white man thinks his beast is just a horse. He only believes this because he has never looked into the eyes of my horse before we ride into battle."* The Indians have many tales of animal spirits. The legend of the bear: The bear was a symbol of power, but was lazy and fat. The cat was fast and cunning, but not to be trusted. The owl was wise, for it sees all and says very little. Even the buck deer was revered and seen as a symbol of strength. The buck deer instilled in them the idea that the next year would be full of deer to hunt. This meant survival, not a trophy.

We see animals as inferior and something to be controlled, hunted, and sacrificed for all sorts of pathetically ridiculous crap. Maybe if we kill enough of them we can figure out how to live a couple years longer. Maybe if we kill them all we can live long enough to see ourselves die. Maybe we can find the secrets to DNA or cancer by killing animals. Maybe cancer is Mother Nature's answer to the human disease that plagues the Earth.

I don't hate mankind, but sometimes it truly upsets me to consider how overconfident we really are. Life on Earth was not put here for us, and I don't care if you go deer hunting once a year. I like to hunt myself! I only hunt for food! I have no desire to kill anything or anyone, unless there is a good reason. In the military I was trained to kill Russians. Luckily I never had a reason or a need to do so. Our belief on life is partially the basis for my next point. Where are we going in this world, or life? Can we learn to live in a world where we are not the master? What would we do if we weren't? I can't help but think that we are just part of the whole. Hopefully we can figure it out before we kill off our antidote, or our cure.

I am not a profit or some other fortune teller that sees all and knows all, but I do have opinions about the future. As is; I see no good coming for the future. I don't believe that we will be wiped out by nuclear war, but more likely some natural disaster. Even if an all out nuclear war were to break out it would not destroy all of mankind. It would only destroy part of the whole. I know that isn't necessarily good news, but you have to realize that man can rebuild. We just don't have the power to wipe out all of life on earth. There are a lot of people that want us all to believe that at a push of a button we can erase millions of years of evolution. We do have the ability to tear down hundreds of year's worth of construction, and maybe even tear down civilization a bit. We will never by our own hand tear down the existence of human life on Earth. This goes along with the arrogance of man. We are simply not satisfied with the fact that we are here. In fact I believe that is the problem. We are here and we don't know why. So we must have some greater power or value. I think not!

The real power is in nature. Nature has given us everything we have. Soon the bill will come due, and just like a credit card company, Mother Nature will unleash her bill collectors. We have been given a loan and our deposit is non-refundable. Sooner or later we must pay. Unfortunately this colorful metaphor is not all that unreal. We have global warming, earthquakes, volcanoes, diseases, and asteroids in addition to things that we haven't even thought of yet, that can kill us all. I just wonder which one will come first.

An asteroid the size of Manhattan struck the Earth 65 million years ago and killed 75% of all life on the planet. That is but one of the five major extinction events that have happened to the Earth in its 4.5 Billion year history. The one that happened about 200 million years ago wiped out about 90% of all life. The point was further proven when the comet Shoemaker/Levi 9 struck Jupiter on the 16th of July 1994. This event proved conclusively that not only was an impact of an extraterrestrial object possible, but it was likely. An object about the size of an average family car exploded over Tunguska Siberia in 1908 and destroyed hundreds of miles of forest. That same object could have leveled New York in seconds. If Mother Nature is the Earth, then Father Time is the Universe, and neither is something we can control.

As the Bible says: *"And ye shall hear of wars and rumors of wars, let thee not forsake; for nation shall rise against nation, and kingdom against kingdom and brother against brother, and these will come to pass, but the end is not yet, for those who remain true; they will be saved."* (Matthew 24:6-13) For all the hard core religious fanatics out there; why haven't they thought of the fact that God will not allow that to happen? God said that he would never again destroy the Earth, and if you believe in the Bible I say you have to believe that.

All I am saying is that religion states that it won't happen; science says it could happen, and the doomsayer says it will happen. I say it has already begun. When a baby is born it has taken its first step toward death. It is just a matter of time before nature takes its price for life. There is an old saying that goes; "we were born in the past, we wait for the future and today is a present. The present is a gift; maybe we should start treating it like one.

I personally think the comet is coming, or some other outside body of destruction. The asteroid Apophasis will come so near Earth in 2029 that we will be able to see it with the naked eye. That is pretty impressive considering it is only a couple of miles across. Then in 2060 it tries again. There are an estimated 10,000 NEO's (Near Earth Objects) in the Solar System and the number of people looking for them would fit in a single average size room. Many scientists would say that the likelihood of this happening is pretty slim. On the other hand they said cigarette smoking was OK at one time as well. Just because some scientist says it's not going to happen, is generally a good reason to think that it will or at least could. These are just a few thoughts about the future.

How can we build a better world when we are still patting our self on the back for the things we have destroyed? How can we hold our children to higher standards if we won't hold our teachers responsible for those standards? How can we secure our borders when people think that "illegal aliens" haven't committed a crime? How can anyone expect people to respect our government when the only people they are interested in are themselves? How can we expect to obtain world peace, when the only peace we will accept is one that we approve of? How can we have a free country when people are always telling us how to live, think, feel, talk, and believe? How do we obtain the American Dream when day to day life resembles more closely a nightmare?

I have many hopes for myself and for mankind. I fear that they are just hopes. Dreams, fantasies, or unreal fabrication of the mind; hope can be but an aspiration left unfulfilled. Yet I still hope…

Chapter 3

Flawed History

Much of history is written by the victors, but what is
learned and remembered is up to the reader.
History is the best guess based on the evidence available.
The pages of time have been written with the blood of the fallen, if we fail
to listen to the words of the dead, we have no one to blame but ourselves.

Our history books are full of stories and tails of great deeds done by great men and women from ages long gone. History is one of our most valuable assets of knowledge. As the old cliché goes, "how do we expect to know where we are going, if we don't know where we have been?" That sounds simple enough, unless we listen to the flawed history of propaganda. Now I am not talking about my opinion of history, I am going to point out some fundamental mistakes and or omissions to the facts that never seem to get talked about. I love reading, writing, and studying history, but it absolutely puzzles me why some people still believe some of the fake truths that are still printed in some text books and even spoken of in documentaries as fact. Even though there is absolutely no truth to the story at all.

I am going to start with my favorite false history lesson: "Columbus discovered America." I can't understand how or even why anyone still believes such stories. Columbus did discover the Caribbean, Puerto Rico, and Cuban islands in 1492 and in his later voyages he explored and landed in several places in Central America, but never set foot on the

United States of America. There are many things they don't talk about in the history text books that at times I find some what disturbing.

Columbus has always been depicted as an explorer and almost an iconic figure of bravery. Christopher Columbus crossed the Atlantic Ocean not for fame of exploration. He was looking for a faster route to India. Why? What was in India that was so important? Most people would probably point out the ivory and spice trade that in the 14th and 15th centuries was almost legendary. Unfortunately that is only part of the truth. One of the most valuable things to be found in India and the Far East are slaves. That was something that Europe was always in need of.

When Columbus landed in the new world, it had nothing to do with proving the world was round. It was an expedition to acquire slaves and gold for Spain. Why Spain? Simple, nobody else cared; because most thought his proposal of finding a quicker way to the Far East was just too dangerous and unlikely. It may be hard to believe, but 15th century Europe and even most of the known world did know the Earth was round. They just didn't know that the land mass that we call the Americas existed.

Once in the Americas he set forth to the business of capturing slaves and raiding villages and towns for their gold, and quickly made himself very wealthy. Wealthy enough to conduct three more voyages to the new world; or New Spain as he called it. Columbus was made governor of the Santo Domingo and after several years of offending the natives; he found himself at the center of the blame for the troubles of the new world. Christopher Columbus died in 1506 and is buried in the Spain. He died alone and penniless.

So why is he so remembered? I have asked this question several times of teachers, professors, and other people of knowledge. The basic answer that I get is "popular tradition." It seems that if that is what one person was taught, then that is what they want their children to be taught, and to hell with the facts. I also have theorized that it is just simpler to reprint the same falsehoods than change the status quo. After all it is easy to remember the nursery rhyme; "Columbus sailed the ocean blue in fourteen hundred ninety two," and so on. This makes the discovery of the new world easy to remember for children and therefore help perpetuate the lie even further. I say this because even that date is incorrect. Yes Columbus landed in Cuba in 1492, but he was not the first to set foot on the Americas from Europe.

Leif Ericson, son of Erik the Red of Norway sailed to Greenland in the year 1000 AD and some say after a storm was forced off course and landed in a place he called Vinland. This is modern day Newfoundland Canada. He set up a settlement, but did not exploit the new territory. He left the exploitation and enslavement of the natives for people such as Columbus and Cortes. Why don't we publish this type of information in the text books?

I think it has to do with the fact the Leif Ericson was a Viking. We have a hard time accepting when someone or something that we consider to be inferior to us, managed to achieve something before us. A classic example of this is the fact that dogs can be used to detect bombs, drugs, missing persons, dead persons, disease, and even cancer; better than we can. Science will not accept that a mere animal can do anything better than we can, but that is an argument for another chapter.

There is also the theory that the Chinese discovered America in 1421. According to a History Channel program, a man by the name of Gavin Menzies found evidence to support the theory that the Chinese beat Columbus by seventy years. However it has been put forth that they may have been here for centuries before that. Unfortunately that appears to be conjecture for now, but I wonder if it is proven, if anyone would care or change the books.

We generally remember Columbus because he was the first to take advantage of the new lands resources. This makes me wonder who will get the credit for landing on the moon if the only way we get entered into the history books is by exploitation of a new world's resource. Maybe we will be relegated to the dusty pages of history the same as Leif Ericson.

American history is full of misinformed and misleading concepts of history. The flawed history started with who and how America was discovered, as in the example of Christopher Columbus. Let's look at who did discover and settle America. We know that Amerigo Vespucci sailed at the same time as Columbus. He sailed from 1497-1504, and was in fact the first to realize that the Americas were in fact a new world and not part of Asia as Columbus thought. In honor of this fact it was decided to name the new land after him. That is how the name America came to be.

Your average grade school child can tell how we got our name, but ask who the first settlers were. Most would answer; "the pilgrims at

Plymouth 1620." The proper response should be; "Wrong." The island of Roanoke was settled in 1587, and Jamestown in 1607: Both years before the pilgrims. Again this is an example of popular history rather than factual history. Roanoke: I will confess probably was written out of history because of the fact that the colonists disappeared and even today we don't know what happened to them. However James town was a permanent settlement and remained the capital of Virginia until the late 17th century.

Most of the time Plymouth and the pilgrims are remembered because of the tradition we know of as Thanksgiving. The colonists shared food with the natives in the interest of peace and good will. The natives shared food because the colonist were about to starve to death. This exchange of good will probably resulted in the deaths of the natives from small pocks or other disease. I guess our idea of good will has changed over the years. Either way this was a story that got wrote down and told from one generation to another and therefore guaranteeing its place in the minds of children.

Then of course there is the question that my niece once asked. "If we were the first to discover America; were did the natives come from?" That is simple: We weren't the first; we were just the first to profit from coming here. The Clovis people crossed a land bridge in what is today called the Bering Strait, between Alaska and Siberia. The Clovis people migrated across this land bridge about 11,500 years ago. Recently there has been some that have found evidence to suggest that even the Clovis people where not fist, but regardless of who was here first it was not the European people that our history books enjoy promoting. This particular educational event between my niece and I had an unfortunate outcome. She doesn't believe history unless I tell it to her and she will not read anything regarding history because she believes that it is all a lie.

So let's continue with all those things that you thought you knew. We celebrate Independence Day on the 4th of July in remembrance of the year of 1776. That is after all when the United States of America became free; is it not. Again the answer is wrong. The declaration of Independence was written by Benjamin Franklin in 1775 and it took another year to convince the rest of the continental congress to sign it. The one that got signed was written by Thomas Jefferson and finally agreed to by the body of congressmen in 1776, but that is not when we won our freedom. It was just a document that declared to the British that they no longer wanted to be part of England. Much the same as a prisoner telling his jailor he wishes to go free. In other words it is just not that simple. Telling someone what one wishes does not make it so. In the case of the American Revolution this was abundantly clear.

If we didn't win our freedom in 1776 when did we? Was that when it started? No. The revolt started officially on the 19th of April 1775, but can be traced back to the Boston Massacre in 1773. This massacre and some other not so well known events lead to the proverbial straw that broke the camel's back. When the British imposed a tax on our tea, we had enough. The famous Boston Tea Party took place on 16th of December 1773, and less known was repeated on the 7th of March 1774. The colonist dressed up as Indians and raided the ships and killed the crews, and finished by throwing the tea into the harbor.

History remembers these individuals as the sons of liberty. England referred to them as terrorists. We all love the phrase; no taxation without representation. That was the point at all. Most people would be surprised to learn that only about 20 percent of the population supported the revolt and by the year 1779, there were more colonists fighting for the British then there were in Washington's army. The fact is that Washington lost most of the battles in which he was engaged.

The inaccuracies continue to fascinate and astound me. The Battle of Bunker Hill never happened. The battle was actually fought at Breeds Hill, and when Washington crossed the Delaware as depicted in the famous painting, the American flag had not been invented yet. With that all said we finally did win our freedom in 1783 with the signing of the Treaty of Paris. The colonies had won a triumphant victory: According to us. According to British the American Revolution is referred to as the uprising in the new world and their history books claim that it simply became too costly to continue the war.

The American Civil War is no exception to these inaccurate and at times ridiculous assumptions. The Civil War was not fought over slavery. This is probably one of the biggest myths about the war that I hear over and over. The war was fought over the same thing wars are often waged over: money. The north was industrialized and the south was agrarian based economy. The north provides the south with the things that they need. The south provides the north with food. Sounds like an equitable system.

It was until the south realized that technically they were getting the short end of the stick. They simply wanted to be paid more for their goods and open trade to other counties for export. This was further complicated when the north passed a law in 1850 known as the Compromise of 1850 that stated all newly added states would be free to decide the issue of slavery on their own. The south saw this as an infringement on their ability to move west.

The federal government believed that they had the right to control the states. With regards to open trading by the states the north refused, because food was a valuable commodity especially in times of war. If we trade food with other countries we may not have enough in times of need. The south then decided to do exactly what America did less than a hundred years prior. They revolted and declared independence from the north. The civil war was waged from 1861 to 1865 and the issue of slavery wasn't even brought up till toward the end of the war.

The Emancipation Proclamation speech given by Abraham Lincoln in 1863 is often quoted and claimed to be the end of slavery. In fact it was a crafty set of words designed to free the slaves outside the Federal Government. In other words: southern slaves. Basically this was intended to free anyone willing to fight for the North, and they would be granted their freedom after the war.

Later the XIII Amendment ratified in December 1865 abolished forced slavery. Strangely enough this didn't free anyone in California and did not apply to the Chinese slaves. This also only applied to U.S. citizens, and therefore did not apply to most of the slaves. They tried to rectify this in 1868 with the signing of the XVI Amendment. The XVI amendment stated that anyone born in the United States was awarded the right of citizenship. This prevented hereditary slavery, but it didn't stop the slaves from being brought in from other countries. These laws were all signed after the war, after Lincoln died, so the idea that the Civil War was in some way about slavery is false. Slavery was an issue of the war, but not the reason for it.

The argument that the Civil War was over slavery started almost immediately after the war. The argument was created as a political statement to attempt to explain the vast atrocities committed on the battlefield, and to give purpose to the families of the dead. After all it all had to be worth it, for some purpose other than economic gain. In fact the act of slavery continued for years, using political and legal loopholes, such as the Share Croppers and the Convict Lease Law of 1846 that allowed a convicted criminal to be "leased" to an individual for the purpose of labor. In other words, if you needed a slave, all you had to do was to have him convicted of a crime. Then he or she could be rented from the state. In my interpretation as well as many others; this basically stated that the state could still own slaves. This law was not overturned until the 1st of July 1928, believe it or not, that is a fact.

Teddy Roosevelt led the Rough Riders on a charge up San Jon hill. No, he was second in command and San Jon hill was actually a couple of miles away, but the real hill was too hard to pronounce so the news papers of the day inserted the location that we all know. This is just one of the many ridiculous ones and I could not resist. On a more serious note; have you ever wondered how WWII started for the U.S.? Naturally no: We are all well aware of how World War Two started; it started when the Japanese attacked Pearl Harbor. An unprovoked act of aggression that resulted in "a date that will live in infamy" as stated by Franklin D. Roosevelt the following day. Or was it, an unprovoked attack?

That depends greatly on your point of view. When Japan invaded Manchuria, the United States and other countries decided that this was wrong. As a newly emerging super power we were eager to show our strength of will. We started by imposing political sanctions, and when they didn't work we refused to trade with them. Finally when all else failed we had to start to blockade their ports, including the sinking of military vessels and ships carrying military goods. Now most people know that is what really happened, yet it gets very little attention and at times I feel that we don't want to remember that side of it. I believe that it is more convenient for us to prefer to think that because of our unequalled righteousness that it wasn't our fault to begin with, nor could it have had anything to do with our actions, inactions, or interference. If a country were to blockade us, and our children were going hungry and some other government was sinking our ships, I find it hard to believe that we wouldn't do the same thing.

An additional not so well known fact about WWII is the fact that it too was a very unpopular war, at least at the time. The largest protest rally in American history was during WWII at the Capital Building in Washington. When we think of protests and war we think of Vietnam and the sixties. The attack on Pearl Harbor didn't change that completely. The reason this part of history is ignored is simple. We won the war: Americans like to be on the winning side. If we had lost the protesters would have said "I told you so" and in the event we win they refer to themselves as the greatest generation.

This becomes increasingly true in the Vietnam War era. There is always the willingness to be right. The South Vietnamese were being systematically forced into Communism and were asking for help. Apparently it is immoral to kill the innocent aggressors, but to stand in the name of freedom is wrong. Many times I have heard my parents and others refer to their generation as the freedom generation, but they were obviously not in support of other people's freedom. Such as the freedom of the South Vietnamese to choose what form of government they want. The Vietnam War is remembered as a failure, because that is precisely how that generation wants it. It is and has always been my opinion that the only reason we didn't succeed is because of the people at home. We lost politically not militarily.

Another falsehood about the Vietnam War lies in its name and duration. People of that generation frequently refer to it as the Vietnam Conflict. In their opinion it wasn't a war it was a police action, because it was never declared by Congress. They will also tell you that the war lasted eight years. The facts are as follows: The first "combat" troops landed in DaNang in 1962 and we finally pulled out in April of 1975. According to my math that was thirteen years. In my opinion it is always easier to lie to yourself. If you question this just go look at the dates on the Vietnam Memorial.

I'm not done there however. Ever ask yourself were some of our holidays come from? Where did the custom of Halloween come from? How did Christmas come to be? Where did the Christmas tree come from? Who named the days of the week? What about our marriage and burial rituals? These are but a segment of concepts that many people have no idea how or why they come to be. I have a lot of fun showing people how the customs that they grew up with come to be, and what they "really" mean.

My favorite holiday is without a doubt Halloween. There are many origins to the popular holiday, but the most recognized is the Celtic tradition of "Summers End". The festival was the Celtic version of the New Year. This celebration was watched over by a deity by the name of Samhain. Samhain would walk the earth on the night of Summers End and choose those who were to die in the coming year. The citizens would celebrate with large bonfires and would tell tales of the dead from the year prior. Since not all dead spirits were good, it became a custom to dress the children up as ghouls and ghosts for the purpose of fooling Samhain into thinking they were already dead.

The Celts celebrated Summers End for thousands of years before the coming of Christianity. Halloween is the oldest holiday that we still practice. Some claims date it back as far as 4000 BCE. Strangely enough Halloween has been celebrated all over the world for centuries. By around 70 AD the Romans had conquered most of Europe including the Celts. With the Roman tradition of adopting a conquered countries customs, Ireland and England were not spared. The Romans continued the tradition and worshiped a goddess by the name of Pomona. From that point Halloween would continue until the advent of Christianity.

With the coming of Christianity around 609 AD the Pope named the 1st of November All Saints Day, and later still the 2nd of November All Souls Day. The 31st of October then became "All Hallows Eve" and the three days combined were referred to as Hallowmas. With time All Hallows Eve became Halloween. Halloween was the night to remember and prey for the dead. All Saints Day people were to prey for the living and All Souls Day they were supposed to prey for those in Purgatory. Over the centuries the later two were all but forgot: Leaving us with Halloween. The holiday as we know underwent several changes before it became the celebration we know today, but it is still the second most popular holiday after Christmas.

That is however the most popular version of Halloween. It is on the other hand not the only example of the history of the oldest holiday. The Vikings for example had their beliefs pertaining to the Celebration of the Dead. The Vikings being a fierce warrior race of explorers and raiders had a colorful religious view of death. For the Vikings the holiday was actually a ten day celebration, during which they were supposed to pay tribute to all the honored dead. The night of the 31st was the most important night of the celebration in which they celebrated and told the heroic tales of the warriors who have died. They feasted and drank, toasted the gods and prayed for a good coming year.

These are but a couple of examples of the traditions dating back hundreds and thousands of years. The Egyptians, Chinese, Mayan, and virtually every culture in the world somehow knew that the 31st of October was a special day. So even if you don't know why you enjoy it, just remember that you do: Now in the words of Bill and Ted; "Party on dudes." (Movie: Bill and Ted's Excellent Adventure, Directed by; Steve Herek 1989)

Christmas has got to be my least favorite holiday. As you read this you will increasingly understand that I am not very religious. However Christmas isn't my least favorite because of religion. Christmas has its pagan beginnings the same as all holidays. Its beginnings are those of pagan gods and pagan rituals, dating back hundreds of years. It was originally called the midwinter eve. It is also known as the winter solstice and many others.

The 25th of December is not the birthday of Jesus Christ. He was actually born in late April or early May. The date that we are all accustomed too is just an arbitrary day that was chosen by the church in about 800 AD. It is also the date of Charlemagne's coronation. That is at least what most people think. It was in fact chosen on purpose to overlap and distort the origins of pagan beliefs. The Christians did this routinely in the 9th century. By naming Christian holidays and celebrating them on the same day as existing holidays it became easier to convert the masses.

This brings me to the point of were Christmas originally came from. Its earliest pagan beginnings can be traced back to ancient Babylon, ironically in modern day Iraq. The Babylonians worshiped the son of Isis who was the god of fertility. They would pray for a good planting season as well as the wellness of the family and the birth of children.

The Romans too celebrated the holiday before Christianity. For the Romans it was a time of feasting and other forms of gluttony, all of which the church would find offensive. They also worshiped the goddess Saturnilia (the Saturn god of agriculture) for a good growing season.

In Northern Europe they worshiped Mithras, who was the son of the sun god Yule. From which we get the phrase Yuletide. The Vikings too had a midwinter celebration. All of these were practiced for centuries before Christianity decided that it should be theirs.

Virtually the entire holiday that we call Christmas is a fictional bunch of misconstrued pagan beliefs. Most of which, are not remembered or cared about by anyone. The closest we come to honoring the original traditions is in the gluttony that we practice. The act of giving was not originally from one family to another, but rather from the rich to the poor, and from those who have to those who do not. In fact the Christmas dinner that most of us enjoy each and every year was originally set out for the visitors that would go door to door for food. Even early Christians practiced this tradition. Today it is nothing more than a day off work were we get to gorge ourselves on food and open presents.

There are literally dozens of these rituals that we practice every day. Many we do without even knowing that we do them. For example: Why do we bury people in the fashion that we do? Just for the purpose of clarification I am addressing the typical burial. The person in a casket buried six feet beep, with a head stone marker. Ever wonder how this practice started? It started with 16th century and the fear of vampires. Six feet is thought to be deep enough that even a vampire cannot break free. However if he or she does, the head stone marks the end of the grave at which the vampires head can be located. Therefore making it easier to find the head and chop it of if someone is suspected of being a vampire. This is another example of one of those rituals that have nothing what so ever to do with religion, but is still practiced as if it was.

Marriage too has its ancient origins. The Vikings practiced marriage for centuries before Christianity ordained it. The Egyptian Pharos had wives, Joseph was married to Mary, and the Druids practiced marriage three to four thousand years before the birth of Christ. Christians of medieval Europe, being the controlling power simply created laws pertaining to marriage so as to control pagan births and forcibly convert people to Christianity. In other words if a couple wished to be married legally they had to go to a Christian church and therefore convert to Christianity.

Even our days of the week are named after pagan gods and goddesses. The names of the week are: Tuesday (Tyr; Norse God of War), Wednesday (Odin; Norse All father), Thursday (Thor; Norse God of Thunder), and Friday for (Freyja; Norse Goddess of the home), with the remaining named of the Roman Gods. There are just so many things that we think we know that it makes me wonder sometimes how much do we really know.

Then there is the biggest offender of all; Hollywood. We have all seen the "based on a true story movie." The unfortunate part is the fact that when they do that, they take the entire "true" aspects and turn them into entertainment by applying the words "Artist Conception." By the time they are done, the only part of the movie that is true is the idea.

One good example of this is the movie "300" (The Last Stand of the Spartan 300) this movie was released in 2007 as was a loose depiction of the Battle of Thermopylae in 480 BCE.

The true story is a fantastical tale of the deeds of men. Faced with the fact that the Athenians (Modern Greece) would not stand and fight the numerically superior Persian Army led by King Xerxes, Leonidas took matters into his own hands. The Athenian Council forbids the Spartans from engaging the Persians, in favor of surrender. Leonidas assembles his 300 bodyguards and takes them on a "hunt". He musters the support of some of Athens other allies and decides to meet the Persians at the pass of Thermopylae.

The Spartans were natural born warriors. That part of the movie is basically correct. Spartan males had one occupation; warrior. Spartan women had one occupation; to be mothers of warriors. They trained for their tasks their whole life. If one survived long enough they could retire at the age of 60 years. Leonidas knew that if they could hold the pass long enough the Athenians would be able to evacuate the city. Leonidas' 300 and the other couple of thousand all knew that this was a one way trip. Historically speaking the Spartans and allies equaled about 7000, and the Persians according to Herodotus equaled around 250,000.

As I said these were the deeds of great men in horrendous times and they faced their destinies with honor and courage. After the second day of battle the Spartans told all who wished to retreat to do so. All did accept the 300 Spartans. One of Xerxes messengers wrote that he observed the Spartans bathing and polishing their armor. This was taken to mean that the Spartans were preparing to retreat. Xerxes sent a messenger to offer surrender out of respect for their incredible bravery. The Spartans were in fact preparing for their own funerals. They refused the Persian offer and met Xerxes army the following morning leaving none of the Spartans alive.

There is much more to the story then that, but the point is that the movie only touched on a couple of points of fact. Yes the battle was fought between the Spartans and the Persians. Xerxes however was not an androgynous freak like depicted in the movie. The immortals were not half man beasts. They never had armor plated rhinos. They were however sold out by a traitor named Ephialtes. The immortals did exist and Xerxes did take Athens. However it was abandoned and Xerxes was defeated later that year at the Battle of Salamis. The Corinthian

Soldiers screamed the battle cry; "Remember the Spartans." For 2500 years we have.

I don't want to bore with endless history lessons, but when it comes to a movie about something from history I would encourage people to learn the truth and take the movie for what it is. Entertainment! Then there are movies like "Pearl Harbor, Brave Heart, and Titanic that are relegated to the dark dismal corners of the simple pathetic love story. I think the makers of the movie Titanic should have went down with the ship. That is the only way they will gain my respect. Brave Heart could have been a good movie if they would have left the love story out of it. The argument is they have to add parts like that to attract a female audience. If that is true maybe women need to get their heads out of the clouds and realize the truth of stories like that. I just wish Hollywood could realize that the truth is a far greater tale than anything they can make up.

The examples that have been given are based in fact! The quandary sometimes comes when we try to convince people of their legitimacy. This becomes extraordinarily difficult when talking about the Bible. That however is a subject for another chapter. I call these aspects of history flawed history because of how they are taught or even how they are remembered. In a world where we put such a high premium on details, wouldn't it make sense to put a premium on the facts about those details? This is the reason that I dislike Christmas so much. People just stumble through the holiday thinking that it represents something positive and good. The reality is they have missed the entire point. Too many people think it has something to do with shopping and a fat mythical idiot that brings kids presents. Maybe when we stop rewarding ourselves with excess, for no other reason than we can, and start giving to those who can't do it for themselves; then maybe I will care. Until then, believe what you want, spend your money and stop crying about what things cost.

There are so many more things that I could ramble on about, but I think I made my point. There are so many cases where one act or law was instituted for one purpose and had another outcome. The lawmakers and politicians that are responsible for the legislation are all too happy to take credit when it has an unintended positive outcome. The truth in many cases is that they never even thought of that possibility. It happens in reverse as well. A good example of this would be Prohibition. A law intended to reduce improper behavior and reduce crime, had the worst possible opposite effect. With organized crime as big as ever, some would argue that we are still paying for that mistake today. Therefore the truth of the matter is far more important than our simple opinions of the deeds of great men and women of history.

Chapter 4

Marriage and Children

The love of a good woman makes one whole.
Life without that women is death; slow and sure.
Your friends are your family.
For those that are worthy, hold on with all your strength.
There is no substitute for good friends, chose them wisely.

Marriage in metaphoric terms can be referred to as a war of wills, and the only hope of winning, lies in knowing which battles to lose. Just as in combat there are several stages of the battle. We have the reconnaissance stage, then there is the engagement, then the fight is on, and finally there is the cessation of hostilities and finally peace. There are four stages of actions and reactions that lead to a successful and happy marriage. That's not to say that all actions will seem logical. In fact most will seem anything but logical. That is the nature of the game. OH, but what a game it is.

Now before I go on I should point out that I have been married for twenty-plus years, and our relationship is as good and as strong as it has ever been. All of my advice is based on my personal experience and the experience of my friends and their relationships. Now please: if you are reading this for advice on how to have a successful marriage, don't start spewing off about what Larry said would work. It would probably be far more productive if you and your spouse talked about the things I point out. It might even be fun, and if you learn something about each other in the process, then all the better. For the young couple or the single person; I would just like to point out that the things I talk about in this section have taken years of patience, compromise, and arguing. For the women or young ladies I say: We men do get it. For some it takes longer and more work, but we are not all "Dogs'. To the men I say: Learn to just be wrong once and a while, because as long as you're right when it matters, she will love you all the more.

There are tons of books claiming they know the secrets of a successful marriage. This isn't one of them. This part is about what has worked in my life and in my observations. Now as I said a relationship is like a military action. So we will start with the recon part of the action. During any recon you must ascertain the objects strengths and weaknesses. The first thing you need to realize is that they are watching you as well. So one needs to be careful about how they do their recon. If you seem too noticeable or obvious, that might be successful for the one night stand or the quick assault, but it tells you nothing about your target. Take the time to get to know them and mean it. If possible become friends with them.

Now if you do this part right, even if you are not victorious in your endeavor, you may find yourself a friend none the less. I know that's not what you're looking for, but think about what a friend of the opposite sex can provide. If your friend is good looking, rich, or a rock star or whatever it is, it is human nature to hang out with other people that are similar. So even if your first choice doesn't work out, it's OK to be friends. In my case I was friends with my future wife for quite a while before we started dating. She introduced me to all kinds of beautiful sexy women and I slowly became friends with them as well. With time I was constantly surrounded by these hot women and every one had to be thinking what is he doing different. The simple fact of the matter was I did nothing.

There are other things that friends of the opposite sex can provide, such as guidance. They can confirm or deny your dress, hair style, or attitude. For those of you that are going to say: "I do what I want, if they don't like it then to hell with them", I would have to say yes, but whatever that style is will either be successful in the world that you are looking or it won't. Picture if you will, the heavy metal dude going to a church function: you get the idea. If you are the heavy metal dude going to a church function to pick up women, then you are just "wrong." I never even tried that. I'm just saying keep within what you are looking for. Of course that has to do with understanding what it is you are looking for. (Type of person I mean)

The last thing that I have to say about that is the fact is; people need to analyze what exact type of person they are looking for and think they would be happy with. More importantly: not what kind of person they think they can create. It's easy for the teenager to automatically be attracted to the good looking cheerleader or the captain of the football team, but that is just looks. I'm not saying that there isn't a chance of ending up with an attractive person of the opposite sex, but it's the personality and personal interests of that person that will ultimately spell success or failure. Just because the cheerleader is hot, doesn't mean that you are going to have any interest in anything else she does. I mean; what kind of books does she like, or movies, or what are her favorite restaurants. You would be pretty embarrassed if you took her to a steak house and then found out she was a vegetarian. Then there is the fact of figuring out what exactly would she find interesting about you. What woman wants to hear about cars and video games during their whole date?

I don't mean to pick on the guys, but I am one. So it makes more sense for me to address those issues that we find ourselves in. Most of this advice will work for the gals as well. I always thought it funny watching young guys try to prove how manly they are. They don't seem to realize that the gal that they are with already noticed, or she probably would have gone out with him to begin with. She is trying to ascertain whether or not there are any brains to go with the brawn. In my experience women like honesty, and they like to be noticed. Women do put a lot of effort into looking good, it would be a good idea to pay attention to her rather than the cool car that just drove by or what the score of the game is. If the game is that dam important don't go on a date when there is a game.

So in the dating game for the guy, you need to pay attention to her and what she likes. For the gals, you might need to put up with our male egos and our silly games, but with a little patience, you will hopefully find out that there is more going on in that thick skull than sports and cars. It sometimes just takes a while for it to come out. Trust me guys if you pay attention and notice when she changes her hair, or buys a new pair of jeans, or whatever, you will be rewarded for your diligence.

In my opinion you want someone that completes you. No! That is not some romantic crap from the movies. I am dead serious. I was a soldier: aggressive, confident, and never afraid of anything. My wife is strong enough to handle or deal with me, confident in her own right, but she brought intelligence, compassion, and gave my other skills a reason to have. What good is it to be the warrior without a war? A warrior doesn't need a war! A warrior needs something to defend, protect or to sacrifice for; my wife gave me that, and was willing to accept that warrior spirit within me. It's not easy to see someone you care about take chances, but my wife does it like an old pro. She does this because she understands. I'm not sure what I gave her, maybe we will have to wait for her to write a book and see.

I have always believed that is why opposites attract. If you look for someone just like you, then maybe you would be better off looking in the mirror. I have seen relationships such as this many times. The ones in the past didn't work and the ones in the present aren't working so well. For example my one friend is a Type "A" personality and her boyfriend is as well. Guess how well this relationship is working. If she would just realize that she is an anal control freak and look for someone that was OK with that everyone would be happy. Instead she spends most of her time trying to change or fix something that isn't broken. It's just different. It's different in the fact that it's the same. OK, I know that sounds strange, but if you think about it awhile, you will get the idea.

Now once you find that person, that doesn't mean that you're done. In fact the game has just begun. This is the part where you need to adapt, or compromise, assuming this is the one you really want to be with. If you are telling yourself that he or she won't change me, then the relationship is already doomed. For a relationship to work there must be compromise. Metaphorically speaking you can combine to pieces of clay, but you can't combine two rocks. Why? Because the rocks are hard and unchanging, but clay can be molded: Now you can somewhat combine a rock and clay, however it will only change the appearance of the stone, and the clay can easily be stripped away.

The first compromise that you will have to deal with is all the little pet peeves that you will undoubtedly have. You can start by ignoring all the little things. Just because someone leaves the cap off the toothpaste doesn't make them a bad person. If a woman complains about you leaving the toilet seat up, do something about it, it's not an attack on your manhood. It also doesn't mean that you're "on a short leash" because you have common courtesy for your girlfriend. Being kind, and treating people with respect doesn't make you the softy and it certainly doesn't make you less of a man. With time you will learn that it actually makes you more of a man.

Another thing that young couples have problems with is the whole possession concept. Your significant other is not a possession, and the sooner you realize that the better off you will be. Your girlfriend or boyfriend will at some point want to go out with their friends. That doesn't mean they don't want to be with you. When couples first get together it's as if they are joined at the hip. That isn't healthy for the relationship. You will go through this stage, but the earlier that you can get over it the stronger the relationship will become. Separation at times builds trust. Trust is the foundation of all relationships. Without it you have nothing. Trust is such a simple thing to accomplish.

The best way to accomplish this is to start by trusting your partner, and by exhibiting trustworthy behavior. For example if you tell partner that you will be somewhere at 5 o'clock then you better be there at 5 o'clock. If you going to be late for a date or anything that you had planned on doing, call and tell them because when you start living together, this becomes even more important. You decide to stop at the bar on your way home, you need to call at let them know that is what you are doing. This is not asking permission, it is being honest and courteous. There is nothing wrong with being a responsible person. There will be times when you won't be able to stop because your partner has other plans, but it's better to change your plans and keep them happy.

At some point, if you find that special someone, you will get engaged to be married. However before you do that you need to ask yourself a few questions such as; do I really want to spend the rest of my life with person? Do I trust this person? Can I uphold my half of the commitment? I know these are hard questions to answer because none of us are capable of seeing the future, but they are questions that they should ask themselves anyway. I for example have found myself in many situations where if I didn't have a solid and absolute commitment to my wife, I could have screwed this up many times. I can honestly say my wife is worth ten times what any ten blondes could ever give me. No offence ladies, but my wife is all there is for me.

At some stage after that you will be married. Then the fun really begins. There are the honey do lists and the kids, the job, the bills, and the house. Then there will never be time for having fun with your friends. Not true! In fact the good days are finally here. You have a good spouse, friend, lover, and the one person that knows you better than anyone. I would be willing to bet that my wife knows me better than even my own mother. You will have the rest of your life to have fun with that person, and as for your friends and their spouses, they just become part of the family. Maintaining those friendships while you're dating and so forth is very important as well.

The last thing you want to do is take advice from the buddy that is still a bachelor at thirty or the girlfriend that is on her third husband. Part of making the marriage work is communication. Not only with each other, but with other people that are in the same situation as you or people that have already achieved what it is, you hope to achieve. Like I said; there is nothing that the friend that is not married can tell you about how to make it work. They will be the ones that complain the most about you going home early or whatever, but just don't let that bother you. A good example of this is the one friend I have. She got divorced years ago and she is still convinced that all of her female friends should dump their boyfriends or husbands, because she doesn't have fun anymore. She will complain that every time she and the girls go out for fun, they always have to go home early. Then when she is dating she complains because her boyfriend stays out to late. "I can't for the life of me figure out why she can't find the right man."

So how do you make all this work and still love each other when it's all said and done? It may sound like a joke, but I assure you I am serious. Learn to fight! That is the best, most simple secret to a successful marriage. You and your significant other WILL have fights, and disagreements. That is a fact! So how you argue is a very important aspect of your success or failure. What I mean is learn to focus on the subject. Never argue about the past. Don't insult, and always listen. It is also possible to agree to disagree. My wife and I do not agree on everything, but I do understand her point of view.

Next thing that you need to do is admit when you're wrong. Being wrong isn't the end of the world, but failure to give in could be the end of a good marriage. Trust me, if you stay on subject and don't start getting frustrated and start insulting each other you can and will solve the problem. The last thing you need to do is: NEVER try to manipulate the argument. This happens all the time and it just makes the argument worse. When one person starts turning the others words around so that they mean something other than what they meant, you will just cause the argument to escalate. That is not how you solve problems.

Now for some other things that you should never do under any circumstances: I know it sounds obvious, but never cheat. The whole; "I didn't mean for it to happen" thing is just a bunch of crap. I don't care how drunk, or lonely, or upset, or whatever other excuse there is, there is never, never a good reason or even an acceptable reason to cheat on your spouse. If you don't think you can remain faithful, just get a divorce. There is no reason to hurt someone or anyone in that way. Next thing is you should never lie. They say that the truth hurts, but it doesn't hurt as much as living with someone that you can't trust. Now there are times when the colorful white lie is necessary. For example when she asks if you like what she did to her hair; your answer should always be; "Yes" Whether you know what she did to it or not. Clothes NEVER make a woman look fat.

The women in our lives make our lives worth having, I don't think it's too much to ask that we notice and compliment our wives once and a while. My wife isn't a supper model, but no super model could ever make me as happy as Dena does, and yes I do think she is beautiful. Now for some things that you guys need to do. I have made plenty of suggestions about what not to do, and for the average person with a little common sense, they should be relatively obvious. Some of the things that we guys should do aren't necessarily as transparent.

It may seem silly, but remembering her birthday and your anniversary is very important to a woman. You can forget all other dates but, those two and Valentine's Day are the ones you can never forget. Always kiss your wife before you go to work and when you get home. Make sure to ask her about her day. Another thing that I used to like to do back when my wife still had her job was to send her flowers a couple of times a year with a card that says; "just thinking of you." The important part isn't that you sent her flowers; it's that you sent them to work where the other women in the office can see them and be jealous. Trust me it works, and she will love you for it.

Many times it is all those little things that you don't think would be all that big of a deal that will have the best results. Many times it's not the act or the price of the object that she will care about, it is more the emotion that comes with it. This is also true when buying gifts, unless she is a gold digger. Women don't like gift cards, unless of course it's for a salon or for cloths, which is another thing men shouldn't do and that is, not to buy clothes for your wife. It will never fit right, it won't look right, or she just won't like it. Many women also like things that are practical, such as a potted plant rather than flowers. The plant will live for a long time, were as the flowers will only last for a few days. It's the thought that goes into the gift, and not the gift itself that is important and sometimes just the fact that you remembered the date of special significance.

I have spent a fare amount of time talking about what men should or shouldn't do for women. So it's probably only fare that I spend a little bit of time giving advice to the ladies. I'll start with some of those pet peeves that many men have with women, and hopefully some useful solutions to those things that irritate us so much. The first one that comes to mind is the never ending questions with no right answer. A good one is when my wife will ask me if her outfit looks OK. There are two possible answers: "Yes dear it looks nice." Then she tells me that I am lying, or I am just saying that to be nice. I could tell her that it looks like crap, but we all know how that would go over. My point is; don't ask if you don't want to hear the answer.

Another good one is when she will say: "We never go anywhere anymore." I ask, "Well where would you like to go?" She then answers, "I don't know; somewhere." Then as I list several places that we could go and she systematically shoots them down for lack of money or the fact that they don't sound like any fun, to her. We finally end up agreeing that there isn't any place that we need or want to go. The next thing I know I am trying to figure out why we just had a 20 minute conversation about nothing. If you want to complain because we don't go anywhere maybe it would be good idea to have a destination or two for suggestions.

The one that simply leaves me puzzled is when women need to talk about something, but we aren't supposed to respond, because they want to fix the problem themselves. When I want to talk just for the purpose of hearing my own voice, I will at least excuse myself and go to the garage and talk to the wall. The wall won't interrupt, I don't need to repeat myself, I don't need to explain anything, and the best thing is that the wall doesn't tell me that I'm being stupid for worrying about silly things that don't matter. When a guy wants to talk about something it is to get suggestions about what to do about a problem or something that is bothering them.

Women need so bad to be heard that sometimes I think they don't even realize what they are saying. It's just the idea that we listen. Like when you're having a heated discussion about something and you respond to a statement before they are done saying it. So many times people will use the same arguments over and over. So sometimes I don't need to hear the whole thing in order to respond, but then they accuse you of not listening. As if the way they say it is going to change the point of view. When you try to explain the fact that you have heard that argument before, they get mad, because now we are accusing them of being predictable. I have personally spent hours arguing about arguing, or how I am supposed to talk. The point of the discussion is to discuss something and argue one point of view or another. It's not a high school debate where each person has one minute to make their case and then the rebuttal. That is not the way the real world works.

The one that I find the most peculiar is the difference of understanding of common words. Take for example the word help. In a man's world the word help means, "Could you give me a hand with this?" In a women's world the word help means, "Come do this for me." At least that is what it means when any of the women I know ask for help. Otherwise how do you explain when you ask your husband to come help mow the lawn and then you go in the house. That's not what helps means.

This is the same thing when women tell men what to do. Now when my wife tells me to go do something and I respond with the phrase, "Yes mame." She gets all upset, because in her opinion it's not like she ordered me to do it, she asked. Again there is a clear difference in the meaning of the word. When you ask someone to do something there is the possibility that they can say no. When my wife "asks" me to do something and I say no she tells me to do it anyway. So why did she ask if she was just going to tell me to do it anyway? If you ask her, it's because she was just hoping that I would do it because she asked. Either way it's an order. When a woman asks you to do something it's an order, and as long as you can handle that you will be fine.

We all know that the differences between men and women are endless, but I think it is important to talk about them and understand that different is not superior or inferior, they are just different. Something that I wish all of you ladies to understand is that at the end of the day 90 percent of everything we do is for you somehow. Men have high levels of confidence and so forth, yet we so badly need to our spouses to be proud of us.

One last thing that a lot of my friends wives have had problems with over the years is that alone time. Women need alone time and if they don't get it they get really cranky. However when men need alone time the women suddenly think that we don't want to be with them, or don't want them around. Men live in the world of the pack, like the wolf. We love our wives and our kids, but we need that male bonding. You want to keep your husband happy, other than with sex, let him have his alone time with his friends, having a beer or six, or whatever. That time with his friends will come back to your benefit in the end. Virtually everything we do is directly or indirectly done to please the women, so when men do something for themselves, maybe you should just let us have our fun.

Many of you may disagree with some or even all of my assessments, but what is important is to talk. Over the years my wife and I have spent hours talking about these types of differences, and because of these discussions I have learned how she thinks and she has learned how I think. Even if these examples aren't accurate to your life style or your experience; learning to talk and learning that having different opinions is not only OK, but is in my opinion a positive thing. Understanding the reasoning behind other people's opinions is a good way to formulate arguments against that point of view. My wife would tell you that is mean, but it's true. The point is simply to understand the other's reasons for their beliefs.

Children are another aspect of marriage that can complicate and bring great joy, yet still takes a lot of work. Now just for the sake of being one hundred percent honest, I have to tell you that my wife and I do not have any children. We made that choice a long time ago. This has been the subject for a lot of discussion in my family as well as with friends. It surprises me sometimes how many people that seem to think that when you get married you are supposed to have kids. I was actually asked one time why we got married if we didn't want kids. I politely explained to the young lady that we were capable of having children before we were married and the choice to get married had nothing to do with children. We love kids as much as anyone else. It's just that our lifestyle doesn't leave much room for kids. Children are a lot of responsibility and it takes lots of money, time, and patience, these are all things that my wife and I don't have an abundance of.

I personally don't understand why people want kids. Most of our friends do have kids and a couple does not. The ones that don't, own their own house and the ones that do rent. All of our friends that have kids are constantly struggling with money, and almost never have time to do anything other than things that have to do with their kids. Several of our friends have kids that are almost old enough to get out of the house. Because of this they have started to act like kids themselves. On the other hand, I have one set of friends in which his girlfriend is constantly talking about her biological clock. Biological my butt! It's all in her head. This is one of those cases where her parents and her siblings have had an influence on her thinking. It was no different for us. My parents and even her mom were convinced that we needed kids, or more importantly they wanted grandkids. In the example of my friend: she believes that somehow Mother Nature is calling, and simply doesn't understand the fact that my wife is ten years older and has never had this biological need.

If you want kids and are prepared for the responsibility then by all means breed away, but I believe it is something that deserves a fair amount of thought. The example that I was just talking about is one such case. They aren't married, he is unemployed at the moment, they rent an apartment, and his divorce isn't even final from his last marriage. I don't think now is the time for kids, and to hell with the biological clock. As the old saying goes, "don't put the cart before the horse."

Too many people today have kids because they think that is what they are supposed to do. All the while, both parents have jobs, and the kids spend their years in daycare and left to their own devices. I'm sorry if this offends anyone but I know people that can't even tell you what their kids' favorite color is. I guess what I'm getting at is I don't think that people spend enough time thinking about whether or not they should have kids.

The last thing that I want to address in this chapter is the in-laws. The in-laws can be a blessing or a pain. In my opinion they are usually a pain. My wife's mom is pretty cool and she doesn't have a dad. I love my nieces and nephews and my brother and sister in-laws, but all families seem to have some sort of strife.

The major thing that I have learned over the years when it comes to family is they are only family until you get married. (In my opinion.) My wife is my family, and my friends are my brothers and sisters. My dogs are our kids and that is just the way it is. I make no apologies for that. The way I look at things, there is enough drama in everyday life without trying to deal with family drama. That doesn't mean that all of us should stop talking to our parents when we get married, in fact I propose quite the opposite. If you are lucky like a couple of my friends and have parents that become your friends after growing up instead of thinking that they are still in charge, then you have the best of both worlds.

Family can be such a complicated subject because of the fact that we have been brain washed into feeling somehow responsible for everything that happens to them. In modern day life children are nothing more than assets. Before anyone starts getting angry with me, look at the facts. We use them as a tax right off, free labor, and in the case of a divorce we use them as a financial bargaining chip. I know of one person that when her daughter turned eighteen and she lost her earned income credit, she acted as if she was screwed. To the point where she talked about adopting a kid so she could get that money. I also know someone that had a panic attack for the same reason because she was going to have to get a full time job.

Then there are the examples of a couple of people that I know. In this situation they are divorced and in both cases the ex-husbands are trying to get custody of the kids. In both cases I have witness and heard the argument that they only reason they want custody is to get out of paying child support. Also in both cases these two women claim that if they lost their child support they would lose their houses. One of them did after her ex lost his job due to downsizing and they cut her child support. Last is the most pathetic of the bunch. I know a woman that after she lost custody of her kids was ordered to pay child support, she then quit her job and moved in with a guy and lives off him and pays nothing. I am not saying that these cases are typical of all women, but they are true. They are just examples of how we use kids for financial benefit. It seems to me that after a pair of people have a child and then provide for them for eighteen years, they are somehow owed the rest of the life.

The reality is that my wife has been taking care of me longer then my parents did. I lived at home for seventeen and I have been with my wife for twenty-two. Simply put, I never asked to be brought into this world. I think it's downright cruel to make someone pay for something they had no choice in. I honestly hope you love your parents, but I just don't think that we should be obligated to do so.

In closing I feel it important to point out that I am not a person that hates children, nor am I against family values. My wife and I both love kids, we simply chose not to have any. I do love my family, I just happen to believe that after someone gets married, their spouse becomes their number one concern. In the case of children: I can't understand how or why our society relegates our most prized possession to just a political or financial tool.

I wish people would learn to plan, talk, and give deep thought to having children before they do. I wish people would just stop using their kids as the reason or excuse for everything. Bottom line: kids are people, not some bargaining chip, and they should not be seen as employees or burdens. The way I see it: You had them, you deal with it. That is what being an adult and making the big decision is all about.

Chapter 5

Science

As long as we question we are free.
A theory does not make a fact.
If we accept something just because someone says
it is so. We have truly learned nothing.

We have many accepted facts in science, but what will tomorrow bring? A hundred years ago many scientists thought that they had all the answers to the great questions of the day. We of course know today that they were wrong about many things. The same was true five hundred years ago as well. How many of the things we think we know today will be proven wrong tomorrow or next year or even in a hundred years? Most scientists don't care! They have already been paid and will most likely be dead before they are proven wrong. There are several things that are accepted facts today, but some of them need to be questioned. One such example is the age of the Sphinx at The Giza Plateau in Egypt. Dr. Robert Schoch (Professor of Science at Boston University) suggested that the Sphinx was weathered by water and not wind, which would make the Sphinx much older than previously thought. He was systematically ridiculed and forced to shut up. Why? Not because he didn't have a valid point, but because this possibility didn't fit nicely into their timeline. This is one example that I will address along with others. I mean only to pose questions and possible answers to some of these theories.

First I would like to discuss my feelings on science itself. It's my belief as well as understanding that science is the search for truth. For some reason it appears as if we have come to a day in which science is the art of assumption, denial, and closed mindedness. Once upon a time science was a non-partial, nonpolitical, and open minded group of people that wished nothing more than to seek knowledge. Today it is just business. Too many times I feel that the study of anything is funded by governments and investors that wish for the science to match their preconceived ideas and agendas. In the mean time I personally think that important science and important questions are missed.

Look at how drastically our history would be changed if Dr. Schoch is right? First that would mean that all of the hundreds of people that have been studying Egypt for the last century and a half would have been wrong in some of their assumptions and conclusions. Much of the world once believed that we were the center of the universe, and still someone came forward and challenged the idea. This is all I intend to do in this chapter. I feel that when we question, we should get answers. So I will question and theorize on the many things that don't completely make sense to me. For the experts that will be no big idea, because I am not an expert. Still I am a person that thinks and questions, and maybe I just don't accept just any answer that I am handed. In my opinion it takes more than an important title to make you right.

Simple observation can confound science very easily. Mathematically speaking a Bumble Bee and the Brown Bat do not have enough surface area or enough strength in their wings to gain flight. Yet they do! Einstein once proved that life was impossible, and therefore doesn't exist. I have heard it said many times that science just follows the facts. That is in my opinion a very subjective statement when one considers the fact that most of science is based on theory. In other words many times they don't have any facts to follow. I guess it's a good thing that scientists study theories and police detectives study clues and hints, which lead to convictions. If science were to attempt to solve a crime they would start by analyzing whether or not a crime happened, and because eyewitnesses are not credible they would probably tell us that most crimes never happened. Much of science will not accept anything unless they can hold it, touch it, pick it apart, and thoroughly examine every aspect of it. Yet they subscribe to some of the most outlandish theories, and call them facts. I know that it sounds as if I am rambling, but I want you the reader to understand the straight forward common sense point of view that I bring to some of the questions that I will analyze.

If I am going to examine these outlandish theories that I mentioned, it only seems natural that we start at the beginning. Maybe I am wrong, but I cannot believe that I am the only person to ever question the Big Bang Theory. Still, every time I even make a joke about it I am given the answer that it's a fact. If it's a fact; why is it called a theory? The only fact here is that it can't be proven, one way or another. No matter how you look at it there will never be a conclusive positive answer to such questions. We weren't there and as far as we know there was no one around to record the event. Therefore it will always be a theory.

The Big Bang has always intrigued me because of the utterly unbelievable nature of the proposal. The theory holds that the universe was created one day when the planets and galaxies all resided in a single little mass called a singularity. Then after an unknown period of time and for some reason that they cannot explain, it exploded. All of this matter, and molecules, slowly coalesced to form the galaxies and the planets and all of the heavens. What they are trying to say is: First there was nothing, then a Big Bang accrued, and here we are. Sounds wonderfully simple: Unless one starts to think about it.

Now as I have already stated I am not an expert on astronomy, but what I do know is; how to blow things up. With a background in the military and as a performing musician, I can say that my knowledge of pyrotechnics is at least adequate. If I am to assume the universe came to life when this singularity simply blew up. Who triggered the detonation? Nothing that I am aware of is capable of simply exploding on its own accord. It needs an ignition source, a catalyst, and an accelerant to create an explosion.

For example; if you take, say a pound of gun powder and just poor it out on a table, then place a book of matches next to it, and finally set a container of some kind near them both, combined with a short fuse, you will have the components for a bomb. Now these four items can lay idol on the table for hours, days, weeks, or years and nothing will happen. You could even randomly combine the objects and leave then idol again, and still nothing will happen. If one were however combine them in the correct order, then you have a bomb. However it still has no ability to ignite itself. It still requires someone to strike the match. So even with all of the correct components assembled correctly, it still requires an outside force to cause the explosion. So I ask again; who triggered the detonation?

Before any of my critics get the chance; yes there are things in nature that explode without a person assisting it. We have volcanoes, supernovas, and spontaneous combustion, most of which we don't know much about either. I would argue that it still requires a specific set of circumstances, to take place in a specific order to have an explosion possible. Magma that is close to the surface generally doesn't explode, but if it is deep and builds up enough pressure, then it will erupt in a more catastrophic fashion.

Now that I have attacked the idea of this "Big Bang" I want to ask the question; what about the singularity to begin with? Where did it come from? What caused it to exist? What was around the singularity, or was it just empty space? Were there others? It's just difficult for me to believe that everything that we can see in the night's sky somehow all came from this thing that is smaller than an atom. Unless of course, we theorize the existence of a higher power: maybe God? That is simply not acceptable for me. The Big Bang actually makes more sense than God does for me, but that certainly doesn't mean that I agree. Stephen Hawking once suggested that if the Big Bang is true, that it would prove the existence of God, because we know that we cannot create something from nothing.

My simple belief is that the universe has always been here. It expands and shrinks, galaxies are born and then die, and the natural cycle is complete. I realize that trying to understand how something could have just always been is hard, but I would argue that it is no more difficult to understand then the Big Bang.

This brings me to the age of the universe. It would make sense to me that if we knew where the Big Bang happened we could somehow measure the distance and calculate the age of the universe. Oddly they don't know where that happened, how it happened, and therefore do not know when it happened. When it comes to the age of the universe, what we really have is a group of people sitting around agreeing with each other then telling us that they know everything, because they are so smart. It's my opinion that they don't have any clue to the age of the universe. I have never seen, read, or heard even one piece of evidence that shows me that they know what they are talking about.

If the universe is in fact 15 billion years old, what will happen when we photograph an image of a galaxy 16, 17, 18 billion, or more light years away? If the universe is 15 billion years old, we should at some point find just an empty void. That is however not what we find. I have seen images released by NASA's Hubble Telescope that show entire galaxies fully formed, and even in their final death throws. It's my understanding that the farther out we look the farther back in time we are looking. If these galaxies are as they appeared billions of years ago, when were they created? I mean if we see a galaxy 15 billion light years away, aren't we seeing that galaxy at the time the singularity exploded? Then there is the problem. It couldn't have been there; in fact it could not have been fully developed at or before the singularity exploded. How do we explain that?

There are a couple of relatively simple solutions to that question. One: They are just wrong on the age. Two: They don't know what they are talking about. Maybe there method for measuring the distance is wrong. Maybe we just don't know, and they can't accept the fact that they don't. As I have previously stated; I feel that it has always been here, and always will.

At this point we will address some questions closer to home. I am of course talking about our home planet of Earth. According to science the Earth is 4.5 billion years old. I have heard several theories about how this time frame was chosen, and I must say that I guess I don't really have any issues with this estimate. I know all of the science community will be happy that I approve of this age for the planet. I do however question some of the details of the assumptions.

The death of the dinosaurs for example has given me reason to question several things. Now I do believe that an asteroid killed off the dinosaurs, but I'm not sure that I agree with the order of events. I have always believed that there was something else going on. Perhaps climate change, or disease, or any of a thousand other reasons could have started their demise. I feel that the asteroid strike simple put the last nail in the coffin for the dinosaurs. This is evident to me because there are little or no fossils of dinosaurs above the KT boundary. If the asteroid killed the dinosaurs in one catastrophic event, the fossils should be above the KT boundary and not below. The majority of the fossils exist in the lower levels meaning that they were dead long before the asteroid hit. Or were they?

When the asteroid impacted Chicxulub, billions of tons of earth and debris would have been discharged. I surmise that due to the nature of this impact, [meaning the size] this debris would have been thrown high into the atmosphere. In fact I believe that it was thrown higher than we think. If this debris was ejected high enough, it may have even entered a low Earth orbit in the upper stratosphere. There it just lingered for decades, possibly longer, or maybe a lot longer.

What if the debris cloud lingered in the upper stratosphere for hundreds or thousands of years? This cloud would have made the earth cold, dark, and unable of sustaining life. However the cloud could not hang there forever. It would eventually start to rain back to earth. By the time the debris cloud started to rain back to Earth many of the animals that lived before the impact would now be dead. This could explain why there are fossils above the KT Boundary.

I do not suggest that either one of these examples are true, but rather that they could be true. We will never know for sure and that leaves lots of room for speculation and theories.

I feel that this type of thinking can be applied to our understanding of evolution as well. I mentioned in an earlier chapter that I believed that our evolution was more accident then with purpose. I believe that our understanding of evolution is about as incomplete as our understanding of the universe. The only way we will ever hope to understand such things will be to stop thinking that we are it, or that somehow we are the end result. A simple set of haphazard events caused a group of individuals to harness the use of fire and make tools. I personally think that given the correct set of circumstances any species could and would replace man as the top of the food chain. Granted we will never allow that to happen, as long as we are here, but I do think it is possible. To believe anything else is to put ourselves above all else.

This is the same thinking that I apply to some of our ancient civilizations. I already mentioned Dr. Schoch and his beliefs on the pyramids of Egypt. I ask: why is it so hard to believe that there could have been a highly developed, sophisticated society in the Neolithic period or even before. There are actually several examples of cultures and societies that could have existed before the Egyptians. The ruins at Puma Punku and Tiahuanaco of Bolivia have been dated to around twelve thousand years. Which is a full five thousand years before the Egyptians built their legendary pyramids. Now I know that Atlantis is a touchy subject when it comes to science, but Plato wrote that it was destroyed ten thousand years before he wrote about it. This would have put it within a similar time frame as Puma Punku.

Regardless of how one breaks it down several cultures developed, thrived, and died in several locations around the world. With similar fashion to that of Christopher Columbus, the only history that seems to matter is that in which leads to the world we already believe in.

I will elaborate more on the civilization points coming up, but right now I should address how we got there to begin with. Our oldest ancestors apparently decided to walk on two legs about 4 million years ago. These people are referred to as Australopithecus, and they did learn to walk on two legs. Maybe they just had to because of a birth defect, and therefore had no choice. Either way they did.

These adaptations lead too many changes in behavior and life style. For the next 2 million years we tried to figure out how to walk and probably more importantly how to run. Then Homo Habilus came alone, and figured out how to use a stick as a weapon, and a rock as hammer. So looking at it from one point of view; we finally, after 2 million years achieved the intelligence that made us a little smarter than cattle. Why did it take so long? It took so long because we probably spent most our time running away from things that were smarter, faster, and stronger than we were. We did however have one advantage. That is our wonderful opposable thumbs. We could grasp things: this made it possible for us to harness fire, and eventually make tools. Not just use them.

Then for the next 1 ½ million years we struggled with our sticks and stones, while learning to live in family groups and practicing our hunting skills. Homo-Erectus lived in all sorts of places. It appears that they started to migrate to other places such as China and Europe. Finally around 300 thousand years ago we finally figured out how to hunt successfully, adapt to our climate by making cloths, and discovered art in the form of cave drawing. With another 290 thousand years we eventually discovered the means for civilization.

We discovered how to write, and how to record our thoughts and our memories. This was and is probably the single most important event to ever happen in our history. The earliest writings we have discovered were discovered in a place called Ur, in modern day Iraq. It was written by the Sumerians of the Middle East. Their writing is called Cuneiform and was written about 6000 BCE. So in order to put this into perspective, let's pretend that the whole of human history could be condensed to a two hour movie.

The first hour and half would be taken up with us trying to survive a meager existence. Ten minutes later we would master the art of hunting, and learn to draw pictures on cave walls. Then in the last minute, about

40 seconds before the end we would discover writing. With 36 seconds left the pyramids would be built, and finally Columbus would land in the new world 3 seconds before the end. In other words all of what we think of as civilization has been created and realized in the last 40 seconds. Geologically speaking we went from learning to write to landing men on the moon in the blink of an eye. Basically speaking for the first 1:59 minutes and 20 seconds of the movie we had the equivalent intelligence of a child under the age of one, or the average intelligence of any domestic cow.

After 2 million years, we somehow managed to claim control of this world. Even if it has only came to be in the last few thousand years. Does that seem strange to anyone but me? How is it possible that virtually all of our culture, civilization, and knowledge all come to be in the last seconds of a movie? I mean talk about a slow beginning. Here are some of my thoughts on the matter.

Sumerian Cuneiform is the oldest know writing to exist. However it is not the only ancient writing to exist. The ancient land of Egypt had Hieroglyphics, India had Sand script, China had Characters, the Germanic tribes had Runes and even the Americas had their own writings. All distinct, all individual, and all unique, this tells me that they were all developed and created individually and independently of each other. None of these examples have been dated as old as the Sumerian text, but that doesn't mean that it didn't exist. From about 3000 to 6000 BCE it seems that writing cropped up on just about every continent in the world. In the vastness of history and time; this virtually happened simultaneously. With no contact and in some cases separated by oceans, different people developed the same ideas at roughly the same time. How?

This isn't the only development that stands out. We have the apparent interest and ability for megalithic building. The creation of law is typically attributed to Hammurabi, but there is no indication that he was the first or the only one to do such things, he just happened to write it down. (Thanks to the invention of writing.) Beyond all of this is the building and art. The ability to understand architecture, and the pyramid in particular was what seems to be a fantastic fashion statement of the day.

In his book Chariots of the Gods by Erich von Daniken, makes the connection to the fact that pyramids seem to have popped up on several corners of the world. At least four distinctly individual cultures all built pyramidal type structures in ancient times. How and why did they come to the same conclusions at or about the same time, thousands of miles apart? While the pyramids are not the only similarities, they are the most interesting, at least in my opinion. We also have art and a desire for artistic views, such as statues, and a need to make structure desirable, rather than simply functional. Then we have organized religion. Religion probably popped up all over the world at several different times, but the organization of these religions seemed to come about the same time. Now we have the creation of writing, architecture, organized religion, law, and government all around the world. How is this possible?

The simple answer is that it isn't. The Cuneiform tablet that was found in Iraq is just the oldest that we have. They were doing this for centuries, and perhaps millennium before this particular tablet was written. My point is that they didn't all start doing all these things at the same time; they were developed over the ages. There is no proof that the Sumerians were the first to invent writing. Theirs is just the oldest example we have. I feel that the same is true for all the other examples as well. What I am trying to point out is I believe that civilization is older than previously imagined. I do believe that the megalithic builders of ancient times were ingenious and brilliant all at the same time. What I can't believe is that some king suddenly had an idea and they made it work on the first try. They had to be practicing for years, and centuries before. It took us a half a million years to figure out how to hunt successfully, and they want me to believe they figured out how to build the pyramids in a couple of thousand. I say unlikely!

If we search long enough and hard enough, I think we will discover that there were builders and artist that lived and thrived thousands of years before they built the pyramids. I believe that science should take a more serious look at Dr. Schoch's work. In my opinion it could be the holy grail of science. To find a link that explains how they come to be the megalithic builders and artisans that they were. Otherwise maybe we will have to look more serious at the possibility of the alien astronaut theory. This is the feeling that I get when I read their version of the time line. For example I have never heard a satisfactory explanation of the Nazca Lines in Peru.

As time goes on, I predict that we will discover that life popped up all over the world, and the origins of mankind would not be any different. I believe that civilization is much older than we believe it is today. I feel very strongly about the reality that we will contact or be contacted by alien life.

I am going to finish my opinions of science with some of the worst. I am talking about the ones that think they are or can at least play god. I know I have already said that I am not a Christian, but that doesn't mean that I think anyone gets to pretend to be him or her. I will start with my favorite pet peeve. Psychologists! You want to talk about a group of people that think they are above the rest of us: these are the ones to talk about. They think they can get into our heads and discern how and why we do what we do. These are the worst of the bunch. Look at the fact that they get paid to listen to us complain, wine, and bitch about what ever. Then they charge us a couple of hundred dollars per hour to do so. The entire time getting paid for telling us to write in a journal or, some other crap like that; to help us with our problems. This has got to be the greatest scam in history. The last time my wife talked to one; the shrink asked what she could do to help. My wife replied: "Pay my bills, cure my disease, and make this visit free. Then I won't be depressed." You can imagine how well that worked! She accused my wife of being sarcastic. Then my wife said she was serious. They told her to write in her journal and take these pills, and I will need to see you next week. A round and round we go.

According to a friend of mine the object of psychology is to help you help yourself. Brilliant! I figure if I could help myself, what in the hell do I need you for? I have picked on astrologers, archeologists, climatologists, and several others, without much restraint. All these are people that I generally have an enormous amount of respect for. They work hard and are for the most part brilliant in their field. I feel they just lose sight of the goal some times. There are on the other hand the psychologists, of which I really do not like. I mean that just the way that I say it. These people think that they can get inside our heads, then categorize, and label us, all for the purpose of making themselves feel important.

I recently took a class on psychology, primarily because it was required. This was when I realized exactly why I don't like them. Strangely enough that was about the only thing that I learned from the class. What did I learn? I learned that they suffer from an over inflated ego. They not only can tell us what we are thinking, but why we think it. They can tell us what our dreams mean, as if I cared. Behaviorists go one step further. They think they can tell us about what we do as well as why we do them.

It's as if by trying to tell us why we get mad about something that it will somehow get better. Then they will argue that it's not about making it better it's about helping us control our anger. I say if you hate your job and your boss makes you mad, do something about it. You could kick your boss's ass. Quit your job, complain about it, or just put up with it, in the end it doesn't matter. What I can say is that talking about it won't make your boss stop being an asshole, and I guarantee that it won't make your job more likable.

It's the same thing when people go to marriage counseling. Look, if your marriage is so bad that you need counseling, you should just give it up. You're going to go to the session and listen to each other complain about everything that they don't like. I read once that financial trouble was one of the top reasons that people get divorced. Then when they're having trouble they go farther into debt by paying some moron two or three hundred dollars per hour to tell them they are screwed. In my opinion it was this type of thinking that got them into the financial trouble to begin with.

Then there are the people that take their kids to counseling. Our kids won't listen to us anymore. They won't clean up their room, and they're skipping school, and I'll bet they are even having sex, and OH MY GOD: Drugs! They probably are; just the way you did. I always suspected this the whole time I was growing up, but now that I am grown, I know. I have watched several of my friends freak out about the same things that I watched them do fifteen or twenty years ago. If I had a dollar for every time I asked one of my friends about when they lost their virginity, or how old their partner was, followed by asking how old their kids are, (I would be so rich.) followed by: SHUT UP!

I think it is a lot of fun making people remember that they were kids once too. I understand what most parents are saying, when they remark about how they just wish for their kids to not make the same mistake as they did. I have made hundreds of mistakes, and will probably make more. Those mistakes made me who and what I am, and had I never made those mistakes I wouldn't have the benefit of the first hand knowledge of the experience. There are several things that I have done and seen in my life that I wouldn't wish on anyone, but I wouldn't trade them either. To say nothing of the fact; when was the last time you took the advice from someone who had never experienced what they were giving you advice about. Picture if you will that friend that has been divorced three times trying to give you advice about marriage.

Now that I have completely upset every psychologist in the world that reads this, I will pick on somebody else. The people that wish to manipulate the structure of life itself: Genetics. This is the most over stated and unnecessary science that we have. To try to manipulate the genetic makeup of anything is just asking for trouble, and is in my opinion the same as playing God. We have done this for years, and for the most part failed to produce any substantial or significant breakthroughs that will benefit anyone.

We have manipulated plants to produce more food just to find out that they are more susceptible to disease, or are bad for people, because of some side effect. Look at the technology that we have created in the past. With the idea of saving our crops we developed pesticides. Those pesticides caused cancer for the people spraying them. Caused birth defects and other abnormalities for the people ate the food produced. Finally this development opened the door for chemical warfare. Many would argue that we have made them much better then back then, but I would point out that countries have gotten better at making chemicals as well. It just doesn't make sense to me to kill ten to save ten.

What if we do achieve perfection of such science; what then? Maybe we can have a made to order baby, or maybe if we disagree with how some people think we can just alter their genetic makeup so that they agree with us. We could make everyone beautiful, smart, and perfect in every way. Then we can make them live till they are a hundred and fifty or whatever. It's my personal opinion that no matter how much someone thinks this will help things; it will ultimately do more harm than good. A good example of this lies in the fact that the harder we try to cure the flu the more resilient it becomes. I fear that one day it will mutate to become something that will kill millions instead of thousands. When that day comes the people that funded and preformed the research on these types of things should be held accountable, and punished with all that the law will allow.

Before that day comes we can manipulate, control, and design people just how we want. Take cloning for example: If anyone really thinks that it will never be used to clone people, they are just naive. So we start by genetically enhancing a baby to be strong, fast, intelligent, and healthy. Then we start training them from birth to be soldiers, officers, and to obey. Sound impossible? The Russians under Stalin attempted to cross the genes of a person and an ape to create an enhanced soldier. This isn't science fiction, it is science fact. People need to remember that just because they might find something wrong, that doesn't necessarily mean the rest of the world does.

There are some scientific studies done in this area that is potentially helpful, but too many people find it to be wrong, and that is stem cell research. Using stem cells to cure disease, and help fix missing or lost limbs, and correct birth defects makes perfect sense to me. Unfortunately many people find this to be wrong, yet it is somehow acceptable butcher lab animals so we can cure the common cold. I consider stem cell research to be natural medicine of a sort. Just another example of mans arrogance. In our quest to fix everything we will probably destroy it all.

I thought about dedicating a whole chapter to the subject of Global Warming, but decided that not even I wanted to rant and rave about it that long. I do on the other hand have several questions about the how and why of the subject. Global Warming is a phenomenon that has taken hold of industry, government, and common sense. You simply cannot expect me to believe that man has the ability to affect the entire planet on such a global scale. (No pun intended) If we did create this problem, it has taken two to three hundred years of industrialization to do so. Now we are going to fix it in a decade or two. Not likely.

Since this chapter is supposed to be about science, let's look at the science of Global Warming. I have already stated that I think the Earth is getting warmer; I'm just not convinced of the science behind the cause or the cure. Scientist are great at documenting, classifying, and recording things, they aren't in my opinion all that great at fixing things. I personally have known a couple of scientist that can fill a white board with equations, but couldn't change their own oil in their car, or even change a flat tire.

They are always claiming that; yes the Earth has warmed before, but not this fast. Even if they know that for a fact, why does that mean that it can't? Either way, I feel that we are going to have to deal with it. The Earth is getting warmer, and climate change is coming. What we need to do is prepare. Arguing about how it happened isn't going to fix anything. I have a hard time believing that even if we could definitely say what caused it. I doubt that this conclusion will somehow help fix it, assuming we can "fix it".

There are literally volumes of evidence to prove that this has happened many times before, and it will come. For example: I recently watched a program on the history channel and they were talking about how the Sahara Desert was under water as recently as 10 to 13 thousand years ago. How could one of the driest places on Earth be under water? The climate was probably warmer and therefore the oceans were deeper. While drilling for core samples in Antarctica they found that it was not only much warmer in the past, but it was covered with plants and animals. It has happened before. The only difference is that we weren't packed into our precious cities on the coasts of the world. At least not like today.

This brings me to why it has become such a big deal. I don't think that anyone really believes that we are going to destroy the planet. The reality is things are going to get uncomfortable compared the way we like them to be. If we believe what they have been claiming for years, one would have no choice but conclude that the Earth is an ever changing planet. To assume that just because we like it this way that it won't change is just pathetic. As I have already said: I think that the Earth is getting warmer.

I believe that reducing pollution, cleaning up our environment, and cleaner more affordable energy is not only necessary, but the right thing to do. Let's not fool ourselves into thinking that we can stop this from happening. At some point we need to grow up and deal with it. Water levels are going to rise, animals will become extinct, and our maps as they exist today will all be incorrect probably in our lifetime. That we cannot change! Change is one of those things that we simply need to get better at.

One way or another change is precisely what we will do. Either on purpose or by accident, it will happen. We will fail to prevent Global Warming. Hopefully we learn to live smarter and cleaner, but I doubt it. We will witness major changes in the years to come. Some will be our futile attempt to fix things that we can't control. Some will be the world trying to adapt to things beyond our understanding. We simply need to resolve ourselves to these basic ideas and get ready for the inevitable.

Can you imagine how things will change when we discover and make contact with life on other worlds? What would happen if we discovered and made contact with a race of people that were thousands or millions of years older than we are? There are people out there that will just say that it will never happen. It's always nice to just bury our heads in the sand, but the fact is we will make contact someday.

The mathematical probability of there being a more advance civilization out there somewhere is close to a hundred percent. If we believe that the universe is 15 billion years old, we also have to believe in the possibility that there are races out there that are much older than we are. Imagine going back in time and try telling the Egyptians how to build the pyramids. Or worse: them telling us how to perform some medical procedure. The differences would be profound in the slightest. However we are only talking about a few thousand years difference. What would that difference look like, if we were communicating with a race that was a million or a billion years older? Their understanding of the universe would undoubtedly be different than ours.

What if that understanding meant that they could prove that there was no god, or worse that god was an alien? What if we found out that we were just a science project or we started out as an alien prison colony? We must accept the fact that we aren't alone, and all that we know might not be what is right.

We also should speculate as to how and why we possibly made contact. The concept that they are more advanced than we are doesn't mean that they are more civilized. I would argue that it is far more likely that if another planet made contact with us, it probably isn't to see what kinds of things we know. When a more advance race or culture encounters a less advance group of people there is a push to enlighten them: Many times by force if necessary. I can't think of one time in history where we ever helped an inferior race because they wanted it. We have two standard procedures when it comes to contact with inferior groups of people. One: we enlighten them and force them to be like we are. Two: we exploit them and their resources for our own needs. In either case they cease to exist. I mean when was the last time you saw a Native American riding free on the plains hunting buffalo? As much as I encourage people to embrace change there are simply some things that will never change.

Some would suggest that maybe they will be more civilized, and not have the same greed based life style that we have. I can agree with this up to a point. Most if not all of the animal kingdom live within their own species in relative peace and mutual respect, and they have had millions of years to perfect it. However they don't search out other species to make contact with either. They are generally happy just to live in their territory and be left alone. It appears as a species becomes more intelligent they become more controlling of others. When we encounter a more advanced culture than us, I wonder who will be controlling whom.

Then there is the study of DNA. This not only holds the secrets of the universe, but we can lock people in prison for years. For those that deserve it, I say lock them up forever or get rid of them. That is a discussion for a different chapter. Now maybe it is just me, but it seems as if every time I turn around they are letting someone go free because "new" DNA evidence proves that they didn't do it. In some of these cases the only real evidence against them was DNA evidence. First we use it to convict, then we use it to free. Scientists have argued that the science was not perfected or the evidence was contaminated, or some other crap like that. What they are really saying is that they were wrong! Then what happens in another twenty years when we find out that methods we use now are wrong?

I recently watched a program on the History Channel about Bigfoot. The scientific DNA expert on the program made the claim that unless the DNA was retrieved under laboratory conditions he could not certify whether or not the results were accurate. If that is true then all of the people that have rapped or killed someone in a lab are screwed, as for the rest they apparently can't certify the tests accuracy. Either the science is right or it is not: no exceptions.

So what does it all mean? What is the point to this chapter? The fact of the matter is I have the utmost and greatest respect for scientists. They do important hard work, they just need to remember why it is that they are scientist instead of business people. I have several scientists as friends, and we enjoy debating some of these points. My problem with most of these "facts" that I have brought up is the reality that they are theories, and not fact. You can't just take a good idea or some evidence and call it a fact. Whether we are talking about the Big Bang or DNA, no one can say definitively that this or that or the other thing is "fact". In a court of law there can be no room for mistakes, yet we make them and come up with excuses for why. The why is simple! We messed up; we were wrong! At some point science must get over itself and go back to what they do best. Search for knowledge and truth. The truth is the truth even if it doesn't fit nicely into a theory.

Science is not and should not ever become a religion, but that is exactly how too many of the science community treat it today. If we question; they scoff, when we disagree; they insult our intelligence, and when they can't win an argument they will just say; "It doesn't matter because it is just a fact." If it was a fact there shouldn't be any room for argument. When was the last time someone had a disagreement about the length of the day? When was the last time you overheard an argument about whether or not we were the center of the universe? There are facts and there are theories. We all just need to learn the difference.

Science is such an important endeavor that it should never be relegated to the dismal annals of business or politics. We need science but more importantly we scientist that are willing to look for the truth, no matter where it leads them.

Chapter 6

Politics

We need to learn that right is right, but that
sometimes right isn't what we like.
Honesty, integrity, honor, loyalty, and duty are
the armor and weapons of freedom.
Blood is the currency by which we pay for freedom.
Vigilance and readiness are the investments that help us keep our freedom.
"Politician: A person involved in politics for personal
or party profit." (Webster's)[Go figure]

Politics is a word that should cause a shudder of fear and rage in the backbone and soul of all people that care about the world they live in. Politicians are the scourge of the modern age. They lie, manipulate, cheat, and will literally do anything to get re-elected. It is my honest opinion that they don't care about any of us, just their jobs. I apologize for the negativity, but politicians just drive me nuts. I don't care whether they are Democrats or Republicans or any of the other dozen or so recognized parties, they are all morons and idiots.

Here are some of my reasons for my tendency to affront the indignant and greedy. The government spending policies are about as intelligent as trying to make the wind stop blowing. I guarantee that not one of those idiots run their household finances the way they do in office. This country is going to have to learn to do with less when it comes to government spending. We just can't afford all of these high dollar dream projects. Now I'm not talking about Social Security, law enforcement, national security, or education, but bailing out a bunch of banks, while letting those banks foreclose on millions of people homes is just stupid and in my opinion immoral.

Our government is not the first group of idiots to think that money was made on trees. In fact many different governments have tried to keep people happy, line their pockets, and still build a civilization. We have the wondrous distinction of believing that we invented democracy, and capitalism. The reality is that we live in one of the youngest democracies in history. If democracy is so great, then why has it never lasted? The answer lies within the very thing that capitalism stands for: Greed. Maximize profits while minimizing cost: Such a simple philosophy. Unfortunately for the civilizations of history that failed to realize that one needs to pay for what they want, or want more than they can pay for, found their destinies in the pages of history. The rich simply cannot stand on the backs of the poor forever.

As we have recently experienced with the "Economic Down-Turn" and as we have experienced in the past with the Great Depression, capitalism is great when times are good. When they aren't, they are horrible. The problem is we never plan for preventing problems; we only look for the bright and happy things in life. Part of the problem with capitalism is that when things are good we forget that things are not always so great. Then when someone or anyone tries to pass laws, or regulations to prevent the next catastrophe, they are accused of all sorts of atrocities. Atrocities such as socialism or trying to take over everything in the name of government control. Without "Big Government" we can be free to "Capitalize" on all that we see. Provided we are rich and wish to get richer, and care for no one but our selves. Then again: yes that is the life of a capitalist.

Now I am not hoping for some Bolshevik Revolution or crap like that, I am just trying to say that without regulation and control, the economic problems that we have had in the past "will" happen again. We have gotten ourselves into the greatest debt in history. As President Obama stated in a town hall meeting: *"If we honor our obligations of Medicare, Medicaid, Social Security, and Nation Defense, every other program that exists would have to take a 60 percent cut, just to balance the budget."* Now we all know that we can't afford to cut things such as law enforcement, education, or research on science or disease. So then what? Let's cut the military budget, and then we will still need to cut everything else by about 20 percent. This doesn't leave much for us to cut, and still take care of our obligations.

14 Trillion dollars? Our deficit has gone up from the time Obama took office. I am not blaming the democrats; I am in fact blaming the moron's that live in the land of the free. I say 14 "Trillion" with a question mark. I wrote a paper about our debt, and frankly most people don't believe me. If you add in the financial obligations of Social Security, Medicare, and Medicaid and all the other entitlement programs, the debt actually is estimated to be over 53 trillion.

The point is the fact that there is many, many times more debt than what is reported. The money that we are obligated to spend over the next twenty or so years make our present situation look even bleaker. It is very important that we be able to understand the scope and magnitude of these numbers being talked about. Here is the best example that I can come up with. It takes approximately 181 pennies to equal a pound, so if someone had one trillion pennies it would weigh 5.5 billion pounds. That is equivalent to 2.75 million tons, and if that person wished to cash those pennies in at the bank. It would take 110,000 dump trucks to haul them in one trip. Over a hundred thousand trucks; this must just astound the average person. On the other hand our government throws that amount around as if it's just pocket change.

This out of control spending has to stop, but how do we do that? We can't just cut off Social Security, Medicare, Medicaid, National Defense, or any of our entitlement programs that the country has created over the years. Many would point out foreign spending, military spending, the famous pork projects, and several others. Problem is that people forget about the fact that it's all of the above problems and more. There is no "one" fault for the incredible debt. Equally so; there is no one "solution" to the problem. In my opinion there are options.

Everyone knows that if it costs you two thousand dollars to pay your bills and you only make eighteen hundred, there are two choices. You have to cut spending or increase income; period. I know that sounds very simple, but let's think about it for a bit. First there is the possibility of cutting spending. So what do we cut? There is no one program that we could cut to balance the budget; except possibly Social Security. Before anyone gets all bent out of shape, I am not suggesting that we eliminate SSN. I am just saying that the debt is too large for it to be that simple. The second biggest draw on our budget is the military. As we learned on 9/11 there are still threats in the world that we need to guard against. Bottom line the government does have some things that I feel should be cut, but they aren't going to be enough. We all need law enforcement, education, medicine, and jobs, and as long as we do, it is going to cost money. We need to trim the fat were we can, but that will still leave us with a deficit.

This brings me to choice number two; increase revenue. This of course is even more hotly debated. If we have to raise taxes, people want to know by how much and who will pay them, and who is paying what. Many economists agree that raising taxes is the only way that we are going to get our spending under control, but everyone thinks someone else should flip the bill.

I don't like the idea of raising taxes and having to pay the government more money any more than anyone else. The unfortunate reality is if we want all these incredible benefits provided by the government someone has to pay for them. This is why I support a progressive tax that increases as you increase your income. In other words the rich would be responsible for the greatest portion of the bill. How is that fair? The richer you are the better equipped you are to handle the debt. The people that can afford the taxes are the ones that complain the most. Second, the rich should remember that if the economy fails and the countries debt grows to bankruptcy, they are the ones that will suffer the most.

During the recent recession I watched an interview aired on CNN in which they interviewed two interesting people. One was an investment banker and the other was just an average farmer. [Unfortunately I cannot remember either one's name.] The point of the interview was to examine the different affects of the economic down turn on the public. What I found interesting about the interview was the farmer's reaction. He commented on the fact that he grew his own food, had his own water, everything I own is paid for, and "I don't use banks." So the recession has had little effect on his life. In fact he stated that he "couldn't care less what happened on Wall Street." Needless to say the investment banker was appalled by this guy's reaction, and accused people like him of causing the economic situation. Claiming that people that just pay their bills and "Hoard" money are only helping themselves and don't do anything for the good of the country. I was thinking the same thing about the banks, such as AIG, Washington Mutual, Citi Group, and Morgan Stanly. I say time to pay up RICH GUY, and if you don't like it, quit your job and let somebody else come in that will be more than happy to make ten, twenty, or a hundred times more than they make presently. Ask yourself would you rather make 50,000 dollars and pay 10% taxes or 100,000 dollars at 20% taxes? [Think about it.] If anyone would really turn down the hundred thousand dollar job just because of the higher taxes, then you are the one with a problem.

The next subject that I would like to touch on is the makeup of our political system and the Constitution. I will start by explaining what rights the Constitution doesn't give Americans, because that seems to be the source of much of the controversy and confusion. Many people seem to think that the U.S. Constitution is the same as civil and human rights. They are not!

After 9/11 President Bush enacted a law that allowed for the creation of Homeland Security Agency, and gave them the right to wire tap, and conduct surveillance on American citizens. This brought a flurry of angry citizens that argued that this law was un-constitutional. This and other security issues such as ex-ray screening at air ports and terrorist profiling has brought out the masses that believe that the right to privacy is a Constitutional right. It is not! Nowhere in the Constitution is the right of privacy even mentioned. Many will point out the IV Amendment, regarding illegal search and seizure as implying that this gives the right to privacy. The law protects one's rights within the boundaries of their home. Anything that is discussed or visible to the outside environment is fair game, and therefore not protected.

The IV Amendment refers to your person, and property, not things you say, or write. However the IX Amendment makes reference to the fact that the government can't deny or disparage other rights held by the people. Some would argue that this clearly indicates that is the majority of the public believe that they have a right to something then they do. Unless one considers the fact the large numbers of people believe that they have a right to live outside the law. I'm not accusing anyone of being a bad person, but I know for a fact that every single person reading this has and will break the law at some point. Do people have a right to smoke Marijuana, drive faster than the speed limit, or cheat on their taxes? Regardless of your opinion on any of these examples one should accept the fact that if the IX Amendment is to be interpreted in that way, then the rights we have may have dire consequences.

Then there are the rights that people confuse and argue about. I will start with the I Amendment (Freedom of Religion and Speech). This is considered by many to be the corner stone of our rights. Just look at the reaction anyone has if they feel that their freedom of speech is being denied. We have all witnessed the time when the press has been excluded from some event and then listened to them act as if they have lost their first born. So tell me: When was the last time you saw an advertisement for the K.K.K or Arian Nation? I never have, and I can say honestly that I hope I don't, but don't they have freedom of speech as well? I have seen advertisements for the Bible, but never for the Qur'an.

It is my opinion that we have the freedom of speech so long as we have something to say that people agree with. I have seen commercials supporting gay rights, the right to life, and all sorts of anti war adds. Can you imagine the uproar that would be caused if somebody produce a pro-choice add or an anti-gay commercial? By restricting such things are we not contradicting that which we hold so high? It's my personal belief that political adds should not be allowed on television at all, but if they are going to allow one form of add then they should have to allow the opposing view of that add. I realize that companies such as ABC, NBC, and CBS all have rights to air what they find appropriate, but I do think that by limiting their ads by promoting their corporate view, they are in fact denying freedom of speech to others.

Look at the endless controversy over the II Amendment. I am sorry but anyone capable of reading and understanding the English language should be capable of understanding the fact that we have the right to bear arms. With the exception of some radical left wing extremists I have never been told or read anywhere that the law says any different. Many of them will argue that the II Amendment refers to the "Militia". All you have to do is look up the word militia in the dictionary. According to Webster's it refers to every able bodied male of a town or state. Some would also point out that it refers to the National Guard. This is true, but I find it hard to believe that our founding Fathers would dedicate the second, and not tenth or fifteenth Amendment to a group of people that already existed. It seems utterly stupid to think that our founding Fathers wrote a law that allowed our own standing army the right to have weapons. The "National Guard" was formed in 1739, many decades before the Constitution was written. Then there is the IX Amendment that I mentioned earlier. Most people that I know believe they have the right to own firearms, so they must if you believe the argument made in the name of privacy.

I do not and never will trust our government until they start to run under the only political party that matters. The People's Party! I am so tired of the right and the left, the Democrats, and the Republicans, and the liberals and conservatives that I could just scream. When are these idiots going to realize that we are "One nation with life, liberty, and justice for ALL?" This doesn't mean that I support the "Tea Party" either. The Tea Baggers as I call them are just another group of squeaky wheels, and I hope somebody puts some oil on them soon and shut them up. Protesting and calling the President a Socialist and crying about the deficit doesn't fix anything. The Tea Baggers are only going to divide the country further. As far as I am concerned they are just another special interest group, they aren't interested in America they are just interested in themselves; which makes them the same as what we have.

The last thing that I wish to mock about our government is all of the ridiculous and pathetic political absurdity. I don't know about anyone else, but I am about at the end of my rope with the words; Bi-Partisan and Transparent. It has gotten to the point where it seems that a politician can't open their mouth without using one or both of these words. If you are that interested in working with the other party, maybe you should try doing it instead of talking about it. Both parties would claim that they try, but the other won't work with them. If we had transparency we would all know who was telling the truth.

There is no bi-partisan anything in the government. There are the Democrats opinions, and there are the Republicans opinions. They both want to be the one that is right, and prove that the other is wrong. In the mean time we the American public sit and wait for things to happen. Most of the time by the time anything gets accomplished it is worse than it was before "they fixed it."

Then you have the present situation. President Obama took office with a Democratic majority in both the House and the Senate. He went into his first term with the idea that he didn't need the Republicans. It's my personal opinion that he entered office with the idea that he was going to push anything and everything trough that he wanted, and do so before the mid-term elections. If everything worked right, he would get his way, everything would be great and his place in history would be ensured. Unfortunately neither he nor his advisors pointed out that there was a reason that we all referred to our Congress as the "Do nothing Congress". They also failed to realize that they were not the first to have a majority. President Clinton had a congressional majority and he got nothing done either.

Democrats like to be in charge, they're just afraid to make decisions.

They love to debate and come up with ideas that will make America better, but won't follow thru and make it happen. I feel they do this because they are afraid of what might happen if it doesn't turn out all happy and good. This is why even though President Bush Jr. had the same Democratic Congress; he got pretty much anything he asked for. They are more than willing to support something if they can blame someone else if it goes wrong. Now I am sure if George Carvel was to read this he would have several things to say. I would agree that the Democrats have done positive things, but most if not all will have little effect on my life. The Democrats have many positive programs and policies: if your gay, or support gay marriage, if your pro choice, support gun control, and love to sit on your hands and debate problems rather than do something about them. I simply don't like the endless discussion and inaction of government.

Now to be fair I must say that the Republicans are no better. The Republicans are great at getting things done: if you're a rich business owner or anyone that don't really need any government help. That explains why they support small government. All the people that they care about are rich and don't need any help. The only thing that I will say that I like about the Republicans is their dedication to the U.S. Constitution. Whereas the Democrats seem to think they need to interoperate The U.S. Constitution the Republicans are capable of just reading the document. With the exception of the phrase "Life Liberty, and Justice For all" they seem more than happy to impose their idea of law. They love the I Amendment as long as your Christian, they love freedom of choice as long as you choose to do what they think is right. They are the ultimate champions of the Constitution. Truthfully speaking they are no better at understanding English than the Democrats.

Now I have established the fact that I am completely disgusted with both parties equally, and therefore not prejudice against either one. Let's look at some of the "bi-partisan" crap that they can't fix, get done, or just comprehend. Let's start with health care. I don't care who you are or how rich you are or even what kind of a lifestyle you have; [We all deserve health care that is affordable]. For those who can't afford it, the health care should be free. We have a right to an attorney, even if we murdered someone. Hell we have that same right even if we can afford one. It makes absolutely no sense to me that a terrorist can have a court appointed, tax payer provided attorney, but my wife doesn't deserve health insurance, or some kid with cancer should be left to die because of the cost. What do court appointed attorneys cost us every year?

We are willing to spend billions of dollars per year to defend murderers and then imprison them for decades rather than execute them all because it is the right thing to do. Yet there are people that think that health care don't make sense and will cost too much. We are not willing to condemn a convicted murderer to death, but its O.K. to let someone slowly die because they got sick. I say it is time to re-evaluate; maybe our priorities are as misguided as our government. Then we have Dr. C. Everett Koop former Surgeon General of the United States making a commercial about how he is worried that seniors will lose health benefits if we pass health care reform. A 93 year old man, who was clearly not a general of anything is worried about sucking a couple of more years out of life and the system, while there are children and young adults all over this country dying, losing their homes, and suffering in general because they can't get health care.

There are off course the tea baggers that support the idea of free market health care. So clearly they support the system we have now. Free markets are what have pushed health care prices to an uncontrollable level. This is another example of how badly out of touch these people truly are. They support a system that will do exactly what the one we have already does, and they think that they invented it.

Health Care has become such an overheated subject, and for what? Fear of doing something that makes sense, or fear that we will turn out like other countries? What would it mean if we were to turn out like other countries? I am always hearing about how "terrible" it would be if we had socialized or unified health care. Yet the only people that complain about these other systems are people that have and can afford the crap that we have now. I have yet to see even one person from Canada, England, France, or any other country interviewed to see how "bad" it would be. So I decided to do some checking for myself. I looked at expected life spans of different countries, as well as quality of life, and health coverage.

What I found was that the United States ranks 1st in GDP, but 92nd in wealth distribution. We also rank 37th in quality of care and 10th according to the United Nations Human Development Index (HDI). As I checked the expected life span for different countries, I discovered that several including Canada, England, France, Norway, Japan, and many others that all have an expected life span greater than the United

States. In fact the U.S. has an expected life span of 77.1 years, were as Canada has a life expectancy of 79.4, and Japan at 80.7 years. The most amazing thing that I found was that in all of the mentioned examples, not only did have a longer life expectancy, but they also had universal health care, and a high quality of life according to the U.N. Sounds absolutely "terrible." I'm not a doctor, but might it be possible that these other countries have a longer life expectancy because of health care, and more precisely, preventative care?

Naturally there will undoubtedly be some critic or opponent to health care that would say that if you think it's so great "why don't you move there." This is just another typical political metaphor for "I don't want to talk about it." Politicians love to side step and avoid any question that would make them think. It's my opinion that we as Americans have become so stuck on ourselves that we figure that if we didn't come up with the idea it must be wrong. By copying some other system we would have to admit that "our way" wasn't the best.

Another ridiculous spectacle of political ignorance is the terror trials. Out of some perverted sense of competition for whom gets credit for prosecuting the terror suspects, and therefore saving the free world, our government has decided to try them in Federal Court. The government wants to protect their rights as a human, and give them a fair and impartial trial. Who do they think they are fooling? How many people really give a crap about the "rights" of some terrorist that wants nothing more than to see us all dead? As for the "fair trial", they have got to be kidding.

During a CNN interview with John King, the White House Press Secretary Robert Gibbs stated that *"these terrorist would be brought to justice and they would meet their maker."* Maybe this statement meant something other than the fact that they would die for their crimes, but I thought that a "fair" trial meant that they were innocent until proven guilty. Sounds to me like; Mr. Gibbs has already made up his mind on their guilt or innocence. On the other hand I think most people have, made up their minds; including me.

If we already know they are guilty, which I feel is pretty obvious, then why all the stress over where they are put on trial? As I said; it is all about politics. They don't care about fair, they just care about who gets the credit for convicting them. If the military does handle it; no one will get to watch the trial or make it more political than it already is. I can't believe that our government is going to waste a bunch of taxpayers' money to determine what we all already know. Then there are all the experts on news programs stating how confident they are in the fact that the Federal Courts can handle this situation just fine. Frankly that is just what I am worried about. By the time they plea bargain and strategize the whole thing, they will probably end up in prison under psychological evaluation, and with good behavior be set free in ten to twenty years. It's my opinion that if they get any sentence other than immediate death, whoever is responsible for the sentencing should be brought up on charges of treason.

We then have the insanity of "Don't ask, Don't Tell. With all of our financial problems, people losing their homes, the jobless rate, two wars, and countless other problems to many to mention, the gay community somehow thinks that the most important thing to worry about right now is whether or not they can tell everyone they are gay. Several news programs and other talk shows have brought up the question of how would knowing that these people are gay affect a soldier's ability to do their job. I want to know how telling everyone that they are gay will improve their ability to do their jobs. If it's not going to change their ability to do their job, then I don't see the problem. Either way I see this as a social issue and not a government issue. Therefore our government and congress don't need to be wasting time and money on worrying about whether or not someone can talk openly about their sexual preference.

With all of this futility I couldn't help but to think about some of my favorite idiots. Sarah "Pathetic" Palin is pretty close to the top of my list of people that I hope never gets elected to anything. Every time she opens her mouth I have the almost uncontrollable urge to start breaking things. If she does run for president and somehow wins, I will resign my citizenship, and move to another country.

John "Confused" Kerry Senator of Massachusetts is another one on my list. I call him confused because of his apparent inability to decide whether he supported or hated the Vietnam War. First he joined because it was "the right thing to do" then he protested against the war, and later when he was running for president he claimed that it was necessary. John Kerry is just another example of a politician that will say whatever you want to hear.

Then there is the unforgettable Christen "I'm not a witch" O'Donnell. I'm not sure she is qualified to do laundry. My dog has more knowledge on politics, and my cat is a better expert on foreign affairs. I almost feel bad for the people that have supported her. Then I realized they were probably all witches that have never masturbated and wish to dictate to others how they should live. On second thought: I don't feel sorry for them. All I can say is that I hope and pray that people like O'Donnell never get into office.

The endless insanity of government is not confined to the minds of a few; it is in my opinion engraved in the ideology of the government as a whole. One only needs to look at things such as the Electoral College. The Electoral College has 538 votes that decide the Presidential election; Why? Because that is probably all the higher they are capable of counting. The fact that it even exists has always caused me to question who really elects our leaders. Then there is NASA, the eternal money pit. I love astronomy and always have, but the international space station and the moon are projects that don't benefit anyone living in the real world. Discovering how the moon was created or what materials make up one planetary body or another is fascinating, but it won't help pay anyone's bills or put food on the table. Maybe we will someday find some valuable new energy source on another planet. I think if one exists then maybe the people that will profit from it should be the ones spending the money to find it.

Needless to say, my views on our government aren't very favorable, and they are not likely to change anytime soon. I have come to the conclusion that we need a do over, before it is too late. The reality is; we didn't invent democracy. That existed long before we decided that we should proclaim to take credit for it. The fact is that we live in the longest standing democratic state that has ever existed in history. The Greeks tried it, the Romans, and even the Vikings gave it a shot, but they are all gone.

Why did they fail? They failed because in almost all cases the governments fell, due in part to economic collapse. Revolt is the second largest reason that these governments could not hold out and fell into history. I will discuss this in greater detail in my chapter about economics, but one needs to know that democracy is full of strife and discontent. It can only hold with continued vigilance. National security, social, and economic security is of the utmost importance. We cannot allow greed and unreasonable spending policies create a situation in which our country falls apart.

I wish we could look forward to future of great leaders. People that could learn to govern rather then dabble in the game of politics. At some point we simple must stop governing by popularity. We cannot continue to allow the children to run the household. Equally so we must start to elect leaders that can and will accomplish something, rather than the ones that agree and support ones opinions.

I'm talking about the people that voted for Clinton just because she was a woman, and equally the people that didn't. When people vote for one person over another based entirely on one or two points is helping no one. However, as long as we elect wealthy upper-class people to every office in the nation, we can't expect them to change the status-quo. They are simply all from the same school of thought. The rich look out for the rich.

Chapter 7

Economy

Money is a tool, nothing more.
Tools are used for building. What will you build?
I pledge: I will build an empire; suitable for my wife,
and friends. My dogs shall stand guard.
I love my country, and many years ago I pledged
that I would defend her with my life.
Don't throw it all away.

As I discussed to some degree in the previous chapter, our economy is a complex, and at times almost imposable to understand cluster of numbers and charts. I hope to try and make sense of economics for you as much as for me. While studying for my business degree, economics and financial management was a couple of the hardest subjects for me to learn. For the most part it is just simple math, but if one doesn't put the numbers in the right order then you have a problem. One thing that I will address in this chapter is a theory that I developed while in one of my classes, but first I will try to explain the value and problems with our economy and the function of economics in society.

The concept of economic structure within a country, kingdom, or nation dates back thousands of years. I am not sure who invented economics, but we know that the Egyptians and the Greeks both used taxes to raise capital for the purpose of public spending. Not the same as we think of as public works today, but it was for the public. Now the Egyptians and Greeks didn't use money per say, often taxes was collected in goods, such as cattle or grain. In the 15th century BCE, the

Phoenicians created the coin, or metal currency. Now they didn't do much for economics other than open trade. Being brilliant ship builders and traders the invention of the coin made it easier to count profit and give a designated value for different goods.

Economics and trade are eternally linked. Throughout history nations have used trade to generate money. The money needed for the military, public works, and for the general welfare of the people. Money has been used for building nations for centuries, and today is no different, with the exception that it is much more complicated. We have investors, speculators, Keynesians, Classics, and bankers, to say nothing of Wall Street and all of the overpaid bean counters that work there. We have bears, and bulls, the laissez-faire, and invisible hands with the peaks and troths in our up trends down turns, and our GDP, with GNP, and NAFTA, and at the end of the day I just hope my P/E makes it all worth it and I don't get it in arrears. [It's not supposed to make sense. It should be funny.] In all seriousness, economics is full of terms and charts that takes all of my effort to not make fun of.

The serious side of economics lies in the fact that countries are made, and nations fall based on their ability to understand these seemingly laughable terms. Many countries have tried, and many have failed, and there are even more that we have never heard of because they couldn't manage their economy. Rome for example held the world in the palm of her hand, but failed to manage her money. With time she just got so big and the public needs so great that she just couldn't hold on any longer. Eventually the mighty empire of Rome fell, not to some over powering force, not to natural disaster, or even political strife, even though there was much of that. No: Rome fell to overspending and overwhelming public need. Rome was not the first to learn this lesson and Rome will not be the last. Still in modern times we have seen the collapse of Russia, and there is worry that others may fall as well.

I apologize for the drama and the comedy, but I know how boring economics can be. The best way for me to explain the importance of the Dow Jones Industrial Average is to look at it like a weather prediction. How warm will it get, what will the low be, and when can we expect the next storm. I love the use of metaphors when trying to explain things that are hard for me to understand. The DOW is just a best guess indicator of what investors and other people that are smarter than me think is going to happen in the coming months. We all know that we can't trust the weather man, but it can give you a good idea whether or not you should bring the umbrella to work. If the prediction is right then you're covered, if the prediction is wrong, the umbrella didn't hurt anything.

These predictions can have positive and negative effects. The great depression for example, started with some banks folding up and defaulting on their obligations. Not that different from what happened to Lehman Bro. in 2007. One big and definitely bad event leads to a snowball effect and investors start pulling out their money and the DOW drops, which in turn causes others to do the same, and on and on. Using the weather metaphor, one person gets wet and panics and because nobody else wishes to get wet they just stay indoors. We need to pay attention to what is going on, but we can't panic every time the wind blows. Unfortunately it's not that average everyday person that causes the panic. It is the very people that should know more about it than we do.

As I discussed in the last chapter there are numerous economic challenges for us to address as a nation. The problem is that many of them are things that are needed, and we can't afford them. The first of these that I want to look at is the countries crumbling infrastructure. One thing President Obama plans for the Stimulus package is to invest in our dilapidated highway system. With my brother driving less than a block from crossing the I-35 Bridge in Minneapolis/St. Paul before its collapse, I can say that I agree with the fact that our infrastructure in dire need of a face lift. It has been reported that to fix our infrastructure it will cost 2.2 trillion dollars over the next 5 years, 6 trillion over ten, and an additional 20 trillion dollars by 2050 to modernize and/or replace our infrastructure.

I know there are plenty of people that would say that spending that money would save money in the long run, and they are right. Replacing all the windows on your house, new shingles, and siding will save you money on your energy bill, but if you can't afford to do the upgrades in the first place, then what. Some would argue that we don't need to fix everything right now; maybe we should fix the most important problems. To answer those questions refer to the previous chapter. Who gets to decide what is most important? How do we determine what is most important? The debate would probably outlive the projects that were being proposed. At the end of the day we would probably end up building or repairing a "bridge to nowhere."

There is of course health care, which is estimated that it will cost one trillion dollars. This is one that I disagree with on the cost. How can it cost a trillion dollars to rewrite some legislation? The American public spends many times that per year as is. When you have hospitals making billions of dollars in profits and paying CEO's and doctors millions of dollars in bonuses, then it sounds to me like nothing would change: as far as cost. I firmly believe that there has got to be a better way of administering quality health care at an affordable price. I mean we can split the atom, land a man on the Moon, but we can't agree on health care?

I know that I already beat the subject of health care to death in the last chapter, but I feel that it is one of the more important subjects that we need to address. There are many things that we can arguably put off and let someone else worry about, but health care is not one of them.

I have also already made my opinion known about Global Warming. In this chapter I am going to concentrate on the cost, and viability, rather than the believability. According to some experts going green will cost countries like the United States about 9 trillion dollars over the next five years just to stabilize our emissions. There are no consensus on the cost to start to reverse that damage; assuming we can. Some estimates put it in the hundreds of trillions of dollars over the next century. This is all under the assumption that we can somehow convince countries such as China and India from modernizing and putting up coal plants.

I am all for going green, but as I stated earlier; I would love to update my house with new shingles, windows, and siding and use some high efficiency lights and the whole thing. What people don't think about is what that all cost to do. I would love to go out and buy a new vehicle for my wife and me that gets a hundred miles to the gallon or runs off electricity, but I don't have thirty, forty or fifty thousand dollars laying around. It's as simple as that.

Then there is the incredible military budget, which we have in this country. I hear people complain about how much money we spend on the military, and then I am reminded of 9/11. In the years leading up to 9/11 we had the smallest military budget sense WWI. What did that get us? There have been many analysts that have said that had we maintained the military that we had, and the intelligence gathering forces that we had prior to 9/11, it would not have happened. When our security is in danger everyone loves the fact that we have the most modern and technological military in the world; they just don't want to pay for it. It's like putting in a home security system and thinking it should be free.

This is similar to law enforcement in many ways. We all get mad when we get a fine for speeding, but when they catch the rapist or murderer, and then they are heroes. Heroes that get paid! We like having all these things and people to come to our rescue when we are in trouble, yet we complain about what they get paid or what it all costs. Trying to control the drug traffic in this country costs hundreds of billions of dollars per year, and all we have to do to save that money is stop using. Like that will happen. According to the National Transportation Safety Board; Americans could save about 200 billion dollars per year just obeying traffic laws.

Another good example of this was in a report that came out and reported on CNN that stated that the war in Iraq and Afghanistan cost Americans about 900 billion dollars. Then when I subtract things like their pay, gas, food, uniforms, transportation, and all of the other things that would be getting spent whether we were at war or not; the price dropped significantly. At the end of the day law enforcement, the military, and the fire departments are going to cost money.

I think it would be fabulous to be able to do everything, but unless we figure out how to pay for it, we are going to go without. Then we are left with the question of who, what, and how much are we going to live without? Who gets to decide? How do they go about deciding what is most important? In the examples that I have given; provided that the people that made the estimates are correct; we are looking at about 20 trillion dollars in the next decade or two. We already know that we can't afford that.

Some would say that the technology will get cheaper, more affordable, and easier to implement. Can we wait for technology to catch up? Will it really get cheaper? Technology is developed, distributed, produced, and sold by corporations. Their only goal in a free market society is profit. While we wait, the problems become worse, and the cost to fix them goes up. Classic economists believe that the invisible hand drives the market. It is my fear that the invisible hand will drive us out.

When talking about global warming, overpopulation, our crumbling infrastructures, health care, national security, or the next pandemic, the decisions on who lives, survives and dies will be decided by money. If you don't or can't accept that fact, then you have not lived in America long enough. I love America, and I love free markets, I just hate greed.

To become rich at the expense or the peril of others is criminal. This country was founded on the idea of forming a better union, much like President Obama promised "change that we could believe in." Both have been left to myth, and left unachieved.

Now it is incredibly easy to blame others; so I propose a hypothetical situation. Picture if you can, that you just won 2 trillion dollars in a lottery. After becoming the richest person in the world, you gain incredible political influence worldwide. Because of your wealth and influence the United Nations invites you to a summit. You are asked to discuss what you feel is the most important problems of the world, and they unilaterally vow to match you dollar for dollar for whatever programs that you suggest. I suggest the 2 trillion dollar benchmark, because it is several times that in which any human has ever achieved. What would you choose? How much would you pledge and to what?

Perhaps we could salve starvation. Without social and ethical population control or technology, the population will still continue to rise. Maybe you would spend your money on disease prevention and cures. People then live longer, the need for jobs, food, and space all increase. Would you take care of global warming? We save the planet just too over populate, starve, and kill each other for food. If you fix health care or the infrastructure, the solution becomes nothing more than a band aid, because it will all need to be replaced again in the future. I don't have all the answers, I am just asking you to think about it.

In the last chapter I beat up on the politicians, and that is not exactly my intention in this chapter, however it may seem like it. As I have already over stated, I think the word bi-partisan is a pathetic excuse to try to convince me to think that our government is working together. Other than the word bi-partisan, there is another word that I am sick of hearing. Socialism is a word that politicians love to use when they don't like something, or especially when they think the government is gaining too much control. This is primarily a scare tactic of the Republicans, but I have heard it in many forms, from many places including Democrats.

In the debate about health care, regulatory legislation on the Federal Reserve, or any regulations on business, or social program to help those who can't help themselves, people cry: "Down with the socialists." In the minds of these people: When the government raises taxes they are socialist. When we tell business what they can and can't do; they are socialist. Programs that protect or help the poor are socialist. Restricting business, trade, wages, or hell any law that business doesn't like is socialist.

These complaints come from the same people that: received big bail outs such as, AIG, Citi Group, Washington Mutual, and the American auto industry. The anti-socialists believe in small government: A government in which states are responsible for regulatory legislation and free markets. Yet they think that the key to health care is to take those abilities away from the states and mandate that interstate trade create and control competition among hospitals and the drug companies. They however don't think that we should have to compete against other countries. We can buy drugs for pennies on the dollar from Canada, but that is in their opinion unethical because we don't get to inspect them. In other words we don't profit from them. They believe in free markets as long as the markets we buy from; our own.

The Republicans think that small government is the answer; then you must ask yourself why are they so concerned about things like abortion? Shouldn't that be up to the states and or the individual? Democrats do the same thing with gun control and taxes. The Constitution states that we as citizens have the right to keep and bear arms, but for them that isn't good enough.

In a democratic state we would not have bailed out these big companies. We should not have welfare, unemployment, and everyone that wants an education pays for an education. In a democratic state, if you read the Constitution; is to provide for the national defense and "promote domestic welfare." Not provide it! In fact I believe that every not for profit organization in the country is in conflict with the very concept of capitalism. After all, a not for profit organization can provide services and goods at an unfair competitive price because they aren't trying to earn a profit. If the capitalists had their way, we would pay very little taxes, but the rich would be the only ones with any choices. It is hard to have choices when you are broke.

Frankly I don't give a dam about capitalism, socialism, or any other rich guy's idea of government. Just like any company, the employee is the only reason that the overpaid idiot at the top has a job. Without the blue collar tax payers there is no country. Just ask the Romans. Unfortunately we can't, they got too big for themselves and thought they had all the answers. The only form of government that I believe in is the one that works. I don't care what it is called, what it looks like, or who thought it up, as long as it works. I don't think we are done, and I don't wish to transplant our government with a different one. I just wish we could start to think in the big picture rather than within our narrow party lines, and within our own greed induced vision. I think we are or at least can be better than that.

The concept that we can be better than this was nearly lost in my opinion, when starting in late 2008 our economy started to plummet. In fall of 2007 as I was starting my business degree we were studying the stock market as part of the curriculum. The DOW topped out above 14000 for the first time in history. Then I watched as it lost nearly 60 percent in less than a year, and bottoming out just above 6000. This was incredibly interesting because as we were learning about the stock market and the Federal Reserve, I got to witness the very thing that the Federal Reserve was designed to prevent.

When the economy was good in the 90's there was uncontrolled deregulation, and then President G.W. Bush deregulated even further. Over spending and the inability to care, opened the door for corporate America to do what they do best. Corporate America is like a bunch of teenage kids. Relax the rules, decrease the punishments, and then leave the house unattended with a refrigerator full of alcohol; what do you think will happen. The house will be trashed, god only knows how many would be dead, or in jail, and if the parents are capitalists they would say that it wasn't their fault. The whole time the kids would complain about how unfair it all is. In other words what did they think would happen?

The fact is we have been there before. The Great Depression in 1929 is the one that everyone thinks of, but because it was so long ago everyone thought that; "That will never happen again." [Never?] I am old enough to remember it being said that there would never be an African American President. The fact is we got complacent, and we got caught. As I watched the "Great Recession unfold" I wanted to blame the government, I wanted to blame the banks, and the more I read about it the more I blamed every one. When all is said and done, I do blame the banks and I blame the government for allowing it to happen. I blame the average person that thought everything was fine. I also blame anyone that supported the stimulus and the TARP bail out. As for all the people that supported the bail out and then got upset when the banks gave themselves huge bonuses, I say get a clue.

The real thing that makes me mad is the fact that there were people that predicted this, but no one did anything. There are economists that predicted this down turn years ago. The problem is, and was the fact that no one wanted to listen. Your Classic economists think it will take care of itself. The Keynesians believe that government needs to control and regulate. What do you think? Is it realistic to think that companies can and should be able to do what they want? Under the mythical belief of the invisible hand: they think they can, and should. The invisible hand; in this case has spoken.

It's a great idea that people will always live within their means, and if they don't; they will adjust their behavior. This assumption is based on the concept that people care. Fifty years ago: the idea of bankruptcy, foreclosure, or to just walk away from one's responsibilities was almost sacrilege. There are some today that say it is actually profitable to go "bankrupt." I remember years ago when a banker told me that credit would be the money of the future. Someday money won't exist, and all you will have is credit.

Sadly that day has come. My credit score has things on it that I don't remember, can't trace, and can't even fix. In one example, the company that I supposedly owed money had no record of my debt and no longer existed, yet they refused to take it of my credit score, because I owed them money. The circular argument ensued and I finally told them what I thought of them: "Go F@CK yourself." I can't pay the bill, because it's not on your record? You won't take it off my credit score because it hasn't been paid. "Are you stupid?" Then there was this jackass from the one "un-named company" that had the balls to come to my house and ask me to give them a commitment of "ten" dollars per month. They couldn't tell me what the bill was for, or what service was provided, but they claimed it took place in 1992. The fact was that it was 2007 when they showed up. When I questioned the fact of why so many years had gone by, they claimed that they had tried to get a hold of me. When two guys show up on your door asking for money, or a bank statement, do like I did: refuse everything. It also helps if you have three German Shepherds behind the door. These credit agencies will try anything. Lucky for me: I fear nothing.

Back to the subject! The fact is that there are several people that predicted economic collapse years ago. Just like 9/11, people thought they were just doomsayers. People like things to be positive, and people like to think that our government will save us. They can only save us if they listen to the doomsayers. In the Boy Scouts of America they pride themselves on being prepared. The average American citizen believes being prepared means having enough money to go on vacation. The rest of the time they are content to hope that someone else will take care of whatever happens.

The point that I am trying to get at is: all of the bad things of the last decade (2000-2010) could have been prevented. If only people would have listened to the facts. I myself predicted in 95 that if I were a terrorist and wanted to hurt the U.S I would use a commercial airliner. I was drunk when I said it and it still came true. Have you ever wanted to be wrong? At the time I was told by several insignificant people that there was no threat to America. There will never be a threat, and "it will never happen." Never is a long time!

The great depression was a long time ago. That can "never happen again." We make the same assumptions, same assertions, and the same mistakes, then we tell everyone that this is different. Different idiots: Same situation. In a capitalist society greed is god.

I have a business degree. So how can I feel this way? I believe in free markets, I believe in the chance to be all we can be, and I believe that if people have the chance they will feed you to the dogs. This is too bad, because I like dogs. I believe right is right, good is good, and bad or wrong are avoidable. There are honest businesses out there that work hard to be fair to their employees, customers, and still make a profit. For this country, I think it is time that we start looking for better ways to be those companies. I think that the concept of an honest day's pay for an honest day's work needs to apply to the big shots as well. Example: If you are receiving a 20 million dollar bonus and your employees are getting laid off, losing their home, or just financially struggling, then do you really deserve that bonus?

On the subject of layoffs; I have always been told that there is no "I" in team. Corporate America loves to talk about teamwork, but in my opinion they can't spell the word. I will talk about this subject in greater detail in another chapter but I thought I should make the point, that if a team member is necessary one day, then how can you function properly without them the next? If your favorite football team, were to eliminate their kicker because of budget cuts, and the game comes down to a field goal to decide the championship; it's my guess that you would be pretty disappointed if your team lost because they didn't have their kicker.

We caused or let this happen because of our complacency, now we want to blame someone. This will do no good if we fail to learn from it. Tighter regulations are needed, people have to do with less, and we need to hold our leaders responsible. If we don't there is no future for us or our children.

The enemy is clear. Those who would give in times of excess and take in times of trouble are guilty of the highest of crimes. They will tell you that it is our own fault. They do the same thing! When times are good they leverage themselves as far as the ratios will allow. The problem comes when they make a mistake. When they over estimate the future and assume that things will work in their favor, it's called speculation or forecasting. When we do the same thing it's called living beyond our means. The major difference is in the repercussions of the default. They file Chapter 11 and reorganize. We file Chapter 7 and lose everything.

In the real everyday world of the middle class, blue collar, and the poor; people live in fear of their creditors. The people with the debt live in fear and subservience to those who hold the note. The U.S. owes China, and several other countries trillions of dollars, and AIG and others owe the American people billions. Maybe we should all be afraid, "Very afraid."

I have complained, joked, and assumed! The fact is without question that our economy is in deep trouble. We need to think about the welfare of the whole, and must stop thinking about ourselves. I would love nothing more than to be the richest man on Earth, but what would it matter if the people around me couldn't pay their bills. I would rather be poor, with my honor intact, than be rich with no respect. To any wealthy, spoon up the rectum type people; your money comes from the sweat of others, your freedom comes from the blood of others, and your life is a gift, given by the countless others who have suffered, sweat, bleed, and died for your freedom. DON'T FORGET IT.

If we are to once again come out on top; in the world view: We are going to need to change. Change our views, our ethics (When it come to money), and our policies. If we fail, we will be remembered as just one of those nations that almost made it. Did the Romans, or the Greeks, or even the Russians ever think that their way would fail? No; they thought that they had all the answers, and if everyone worked hard and remained faithful to the counties core values, they would emerge in a world of their design. They would be heralded as the builders of civilization.

For many of these examples that I have provided, the problem was excess. For others doom awaited them in the form of poor management. In this country we suffer from both. Worst of all is the fact that we suffer from an excess of bad management. We work hard, pay our taxes, and hope that our country will do their jobs. They have failed! In the military we were taught that without regard for the person, we must respect the position of our leaders. In my case this was easy. Our leaders worked beside us, slept in the dirt with us, and suffered, fought, and died with us. What do the leaders of our country offer in comparison?

Our leaders talk about how we must tighten our belt, work harder, and believe in them. It's pretty easy to give advice if you are not in a position where you may be forced to suffer the same consequences as those you lead. We have heard countless times about how many of those people that got the sub-prime loans should have never gotten them. What about the idiots that gave them? What about the billions of dollars that these companies made off these "loans" that they should have never given? In my case: we paid over 500.00 per month for twelve years before my wife got sick. This translates into 72,000.00 over twelve years. We paid 31,000.00 dollars for the house, which is 131% of the initial investment on their part. They profit 41,000.00 and think that we are screwing them somehow.

The problem comes not because of those who took out the loans, but those who leveraged that money in the hope that they would profit 200 or 300 percent of their investment. When the housing market fell, due to the jobs market, and the economy in general, these idiots that over extended themselves then decided to blame us. People without jobs, medical conditions, or other unforeseen circumstances, then find themselves unable to pay is, what we call the real world. In the minds of the banker that is a crime. When they do the same thing it is called a bail-out, because somehow they are too important to fail.

At some point these idiots have to grasp the concept that this is a capitalist free market system and failure means the same for them as it does us. If I fail to provide for my family; they go hungry, we lose our home, and we are f@#ked. This should be true for them as well, unless they are thinking of changing the status-quo, and try to think of what is best for the whole instead of what's best for them. The Survivability of a Society Curve is an example of that thinking.

Navigating Insanity

The Survivability of a Society Curve shows that as a society grows, the needs grow at an equal pace. That translates into jobs and growth of the economy. I propose that this model is flawed. In the 19th century it is easy to see how this philosophy came to be. Most things were done the same then as they were two hundred years before. The problem with model lies in the acquisition of technology, innovation, and efficiency. As we improve the way we do things or invent processes that take the place of workers we cause the workers curve to start to fall. With time, there are far more people than there are job. Then we have a problem.

Corporation, businesses, and even not for profit organizations all need the average person to be able to afford their goods or services that they provide. With the rich getting richer, the poor have no choice but to get poorer. In the United States, 80% of everything is owned by 20% of the population. This is the one of the greatest financial separation of wealth in the world. The financial goal of every company in the country is to make that percentage wider. Companies such as AIG, Washington Mutual, Citi Group, (In my opinion) and others would if they had their way make that percentage more like 90/10 or 95/5, and they don't give a rats rectum who or what they have to crush to get there. The principle job of the management of any firm is to maximize profit for the stockholder's. Make the shareholder's happy and to hell with the rest of us. Once upon a time the customer was number one. They all love to tell us that we matter, but I don't think that any of us are really that stupid. Show me one company that thinks that the customer is number one and I will prove that they are lying.

I was once told by my boss that "the company did not exist to provide these people with jobs. If they don't like it, there is the door." If I am ever in a position in which I can change things; I would fire that manager on the spot. To succeed, as I have said we will need to change, and those who will not change will have to go! A wise man once said: "There is no such thing as a free lunch." I wonder if the rich realize this as well.

With remembrance of those things that I hate I think of an organization that I remember reading about many years ago. A friend of mine was associated with a "not for profit" company (That will remain unnamed), whose theme was that enlightenment was more important than the money. Several people that I knew frequently volunteered for this group. Not being a trusting person or someone that believes what people tell me. I didn't believe in the not for profit part of the group.

Frankly it made me mad that people I cared about dedicated hours of time to something in which they received no reward. In their reasoning they would tell me that it was for charity, and that everyone involved was working for the same goal.

Being a person that does not trust so easily; I argued that someone made money off this or it would not exist. We frequently argued and finally got mad at me and said prove it! So I did! I volunteered to be a custodian for the organization. One night when it was just me at the studio, I was cleaning the office. I could not resist! I began looking through their files and financial statements. After reading far enough I approached my friends and asked them if they really thought everyone involved worked for free. Knowing the answer I did not wait for the response. I dropped a photo copy of the file open on the table for them to read, and it showed that a group of people that they had never heard of were receiving many thousands of dollars per year, and even though they thought they were familiar with most of the people involved. They had never even heard of these persons.

They tried to argue that they were probably the primary investors. The books showed that the group was not only self sufficient in the way of reputation, advertising, marketing, and fame that they didn't need these people. When they eventually began to question the fact that no one got paid and that there was all this extra money they got let go. How do you get fired from a company that everyone works on a volunteer basis, and doesn't make any money?

How does a "company" make six figures clear profit per year and pay no one," when many of the people that company are working for them work for free. They do this by following the law and by using every loophole they can find. Not-For-Profit my ass! I personally discovered the books that prove that at least four individuals are making money from a not-for-profit company. Eventually everyone quite, that I cared about. But many of the people that still volunteer for this organization still believe that there is honesty and good in the world.

This example reminds me that people fall for every bullshit idea that comes along. The concept isn't the problem; it's the people involved! There are those that believe and do, there are those that take, and profit. The comparison that I made earlier about the fact that there is no such thing as a free lunch, applies in this case. In other words, this charity would not exist if somebody didn't make money. Many organizations will tell you that they have a right to recover expenses that are incurred in the charity. Funny thing is: When I give money to one of my friends that are losing their home, or can't feed their family; I don't ask for a receipt, and I'm not worried about how it may affect my taxes. I do it because they need it, and because I care.

Just a thought! What if in order to claim a charity on ones taxes, they had to report it to the public? If anyone wanted to claim say $500.00 for PETA they would have to pay for an article in the local news paper. In other words, to get credit for it you would have to make it part of the record. Those who really believe in something and are too embarrassed to report their contribution; then who cares. For those that do; we get to see what kind of people they really are. To this is say: "impress me mother f@#kers." Pardon the French...

I have watched people that have given the last dollar in their wallet, to some cause and not ask for shit. Our economy is based on recognition and responsibility. Just like the organization that I mentioned, they think that as long as people don't know then everything is OK. We just trust that it is all in our best interest. They only interest that they are worried about is their bank accounts, their profit, and what they gain. END OF STORY!!!

Chapter 8

Religion

"It is better to reign in hell than serve in heaven."
God helps those who help themselves is just a convenient
way of saying "you're on your own."
Philosophers have asked what would happen if we could prove
god didn't exist: what if we could prove he or she did.
If it was proven one way or the other would it really change your behavior?

he first thing that I wish to point out in this chapter is that I am not a religious person. I do not however hold judgment on people that are religious. I will bring up some questions that may cause one to believe that I am criticizing them, but I assure you that is not the intention. I just wish to question the logic of some things while pointing out contradictions that I have found in the bible as well as in other religions. Most of which have never been explained to my satisfaction in any way. I have many reasons for why I abandoned religion and I will try to explain those as well.

I will start by explaining why I am not religious. Regardless of what religion you chose to follow, the basic idea that "I" the average everyday person can figure is: I need to live by a good set of morals. A good set of morals? God is a loving god? For those who have faith they will be saved? Saved for what? These are but a few of the bullshit statements that I have heard all my life. If god is so benevolent and loving then why can't he stop what is wrong? "God helps those who help themselves." "Man was given free choice." If free choice gives God the ability to avoid his or her obligations then where do I apply? It must be nice to be omnipotent and all powerful with no responsibility.

As the years passed I watched as friends, one by one died. [Several of them became deceased from automobile accidents, a couple from drugs or suicide, a couple from military action, and even one that was murdered.] Regardless of the reason I can honestly say that they were all good people, and in my opinion deserved to live. Where was this loving, caring and benevolent being when my child hood friend burned to death in his car, on his way home for his 21st birthday. Where was this person when a friend of ours committed suicide after being gang raped? Where was this person when our friend was murdered? It is clear to me that either god exists and doesn't care, or he is not there. In either case what good is he or she?

I was once told that these people were chosen by god to come home early. What a wonderful bunch of crap. It sounds to me as if they are trying to convince themselves, because they definitely aren't convincing me. Some will say; just have faith. True happiness is only found in god's love. I feel perfectly happy, and for the most part have always felt content and satisfied with my life, yet I have never found religion, and have never seriously looked for it. Maybe if you are easily consoled, and can live with the idea that your friends and love ones die because of some great plan, then you are probably OK with religion. I on the other hand feel that death is just that: the end. All the faith in the world can't save you from that.

Maybe it is all in god's plan to allow millions to starve, or die because of genocide, or even through natural catastrophe. I just can't seem to figure out how and why he thinks I should bow to him. If someone were to witness a murder and do nothing to stop it, they would be locked up for their inaction, yet we worship the same kind of inaction, and call it "Gods" will. That somehow makes it all just fine. The bible teaches compassion, kindness, and to love your neighbor, but apparently god doesn't have to live by these rules. "Do as I say, not as I do."

I just refuse to bow to anyone that tells me to do one thing but refuses to practice what they preach. Maybe that is why I hate our politicians? The thing that gets my goat even worse is the fact that three of the largest organized religions are all Christian in origin. Roman Catholics Bible, the Orthodox Jews Torah, and the Islamic Qur'an are all the same story, just from a different point of view. Each in turn will tell you that their version is the correct one. The interesting fact is that they are all incorrect. The oldest religious Christian text that exists was written two hundred years after Jesus lived. All three of the major religions discount this text because it goes against traditional beliefs. Most of those "traditional" beliefs come from a version written centuries later. Even the things we disagree on aren't the truth. I have always been dismayed by the fact that every so called religious person that I have ever met, just picks and chooses which parts they wish to believe, then discount the rest.

All of the things I just mentioned fall into a category that I call the unmentioned and forgotten. Some of these forgotten include: the Dead Sea Scrolls, and the book of Thomas, the book or Enoch and many others. What about the fact that Adam was married twice? Why was the book of Mary cut from the version that you read today? What is hidden in these texts that are so terrible that the average person should be kept in the dark about? The fact is that the church has been manipulating and controlling people lives and reaping the profits from those fears for several millennia. The word of God only matters so long as it can be used to control.

Let's look at the commandments! "Thou shall not kill" (6th Commandment): Sounds great in the fact that it sounds moral and ethical. This commandment went right out the window when it came to witches, werewolves, vampires, and people that spoke blasphemy about the church or anyone in the "employment" of the church. The act of publicly stating that you don't like the local priest could be enough to have yourself hung for blasphemy, or heresy. Hung if you were lucky and confessed, if you didn't confess you may be burned at the stake, or drawn and quartered, or many other gruesome sentences. Thou shall not kill: unless the church says it's OK. That is what it should say.

"I am the lord your god and you shall have no other god before me. (1st Commandment)" This is the commandment that everyone knows, but if you read the whole thing in the Bible it goes on to explains that "I am a jealous god." I thought that was a deadly sin? The Bible also states that we are not to worship or create idols or graven images (2nd Commandment). Have you ever seen a Rosary, Crucifix, or any other religious symbol? The cross on the peak of the church is something that the Bible says is wrong. Yet that is somehow OK because it is the church breaking the rules.

"Thou shall not steal (8th Commandment)!" The concept of protecting property is clearly designed with the rich in mind. If someone breaks into the local convenience store and robs the cash register; that is wrong. When a credit card company decides that they need to increase profit and raise the interest rate on your credit card that is called capitalism and free markets. When they try to take your home because you can't afford to make the payments, they call it justified. I guess it all comes down to your definition of theft.

Remember the Sabbath day to keep it holy! (4th Commandment) This one of my favorites because nobody seems to know when the Sabbath day is. Everyone has been under the misconception that Sunday is the Sabbath for centuries. According to the Bible the Sabbath is the seventh day, the day of rest. Sunday is the first day of the week. That makes Saturday the Sabbath. Problem is nobody wants to rest on Saturday. In pagan times Saturday was time for celebrating the end of the week, and in modern society things have remained relatively the same. The early church decided that Sunday would be easier to get people to rest, since they were probably hung over and needed to repent for the things they did the night before.

For the rest of the commandments you will have to refer to the Bible. Read the rest of them and ask yourself if anyone really obeys these "laws" of god. Or; is it just a convenient set of rules for when people wants to control the actions of others. It's especially convenient when politicians, celebrities or other famous people claim that they are religious then get caught cheating on their spouse. If anyone in this country truly didn't covet anything capitalism would fall. We all know what it means to bear false witness, but we all do it every day. The beauty is that it is all OK because as long as we are sorry for our sins and ask forgiveness everything will be fine. What a wonderfully convenient contradiction in terms and beliefs.

I don't mean to pick on the Christians alone. The Qur'an is no better. The five pillars of Islam aren't really pillars at all. They are more like fence posts, meant to keep people in. The Qur'an preaches charity, worship of god, and that the highest of crimes is to kill a brother of Islam. We have all seen how well those theories have worked out. In much of the Muslim world there is out of control starvation, homelessness, poverty, and death. When suicide bomber blows up some market just to kill a couple of American soldiers, he is breaking the highest law of Allah, and that is the killing of other Muslims.

From that point of view we are all truly the same. We love to preach and control, but as for obeying; we only obey the ones we like. For example: the apocalypse: Revelations is a story of the end of days. Countless people think that it is coming, others believe that god would never let that happen, and still others think it is a metaphor. It's like when people use statistics to prove a point. You can use the same statistics to argue for and against the same idea. If the Bible is the word of god and is truth, then it stands to reason that Armageddon will happen, and the end will come.

People's interpretations aren't the only thing having to do with the Bible that can be contradictory. The Bible itself is full of contradictions and discrepancies that in my opinion can't be ignored. The Bible says that God created the heavens and Earth in seven days. The dinosaurs must have been during the fifth and sixth day, but God forgot to mention them. In fact the Bible doesn't account for a lot of things.

The fact that mankind existed for thousands, and even millions of years before he gave us his only son has been a point of contention for me for years. This all knowing all powerful being created the Earth in seven days: but waited millions of years to enlighten us. Millions of years to send our savior, as I look at the world around me two thousand years after he saved us, and must question what did he save us from?

The Bible says that no living person shall know the names of the angels. We must all be dead, because I for one have heard of Gabriel, Michael, and even Lucifer. Yes Lucifer was an angel, but he attempted to usurp the throne of god and was punished. Either way we know their names.

The greatest forgotten and sometimes unmentioned portion in the bible is all the death and destruction. This grand book of peace and love are full of stories of suffering, pain, war, oppression, but most of all death. If the Bible were made into a full length movie it would probably be rated R for extreme violence. Read the story of the battle of Jericho. King Joshua laid siege to the city of Jericho and when the walls came down he ordered his men to kill all that drew breath. That meant the men, women, children, young, old, and even the livestock. They killed the animals as well as the people; the slaughter went on for days. What was their crime? Put simply they build a city against god, or they refused to worship him.

This has been true through the ages; slaughter in the name of god dates back to the beginning of recorded history. Many of the first writing are depictions of battles in the name of gods. Don't go thinking that it was all just ancient history. The slaughter continued in the 9th century, when Christianity took hold of Europe. The Papal States had existed for a few centuries already at this point but this was when the madness took over. Starting in the late 11th century the Pope decreed that those who would not convert should be destroyed, and so the Armies went forth. For two hundred years the Church waged war against all non-Christian people of the known world. Then in the 16th century the Spanish brought enlightenment to the natives of Central and South America. In the eighteen hundreds we did the same thing to the plains Indians. That still sounds as if it all happened a long time ago.

It still goes on today, just more subdued. Take for example the war in the Middle East; there are many opinions about the why and how of such wars, but I offer this simple solution. We all remember 9/11, and yes I think that is as good of a reason to go to war as any. But let's be clear: What is the war really about if it isn't differing opinions on how people should live and govern? All of those beliefs are rooted in religion; ours and theirs. I feel pretty confident when I say that no other book than the Bible has been the single most cause of death and war in history.

At this point I would like to shift gears so to speak, and dig into the historical relevance of religion and the Bible. Religion has its origins dated in the thousands of years and perhaps even the eons. We don't know what the ancient Neolithic peoples believed, but we do have the early writings in Cuneiform from the ancient settlement of Ur in Samaria. (Modern day Iraq) 8000 years ago people wrote of gods and kings and battles; how and why they chose to write about these things they have not told us.

Irrefutably gods played an important part of early civilized life. Why; because they wrote about them? In fact the very intellectual needs required for such a task should answer the question of the importance. When referring to the ancient Sumerians, it is believed that perhaps one in every thousand people could read, and even less could write. The fact that they would utilize such an important capability means that it was something of cultural and social significance. In other words the gods were important to them. They brought the crops, the rain, and terrible things, in the form of floods, and disease, but either way they brought it.

The early gods were very violent, vengeful, and natural in their composition. There were the gods that regulated the harvest and the rain, but they also regulated birth and death. While trying to please one god, one might offend another and vise verse. The early people worshiped gods such as Anu, the god of the world and father to all, and Tehamat, a seven headed dragon who was the mother of doom. They worshiped thousands of gods with thousands of names. The thousands had one thing in common; they were natural in their complexity; they were Mother Nature. The need to understand the world around them led them in the path of religion.

Who do we blame when bad things happen? Who do we pray to when we hope for the good? Who do we look to when we aren't sure of what direction to go? These are such simple questions, yet they are the ones that have plagued mankind the longest. For thousands of years people, not that different from us have been causing themselves anxiety and suffering trying to answer these among other questions. The gods opened that door! Having a higher power made it much simpler to explain our failings.

It's not all about our failings however. Some gods would emerge to give us hope and guidance. In Egypt there would be Osiris, Phah, and Amun, and in Greece there would be Athena, these were gods that protected the dead, love, fertility, and the Earth itself. They prayed to gods that would protect the family, their crops, and even gods the watched over romance. A god for everything was the basic belief for thousands of years.

Monotheism or the belief in one all powerful god however was not invented by the Christians. The Egyptians for example had the all powerful sun god Ra. For centuries there were many "one god cults" that came and went. Christianity in fact would not even come into the picture until thousands of years later. This brings me to one of those discrepancies in the historical time line.

The Bible tells the story of Moses and the Israelites from about 1300 BCE, and their plight in Egypt as slaves. Historically this has always been attributed to the Pharos Ramses. The first problem I have with this theory is that Dr.Zahi Hawass the Chief of Egyptian Supreme Council of Antiquities in Cairo has proven that the Egyptians did not use slave labor. That's not to say they didn't have slaves, but they were not Jews and they didn't build the temples or pyramids. They were servants, soldiers, and used for everyday life. There has never been any evidence that the slaves, who were from many nations, were mistreated.

Slavery is slavery, but there is no evidence that there was ever a great "Exodus" from Egypt by any group of slaves, and certainly not the 40 thousand that the Bible speaks of. There is not even clear evidence that Christianity existed at the time discussed in the Bible.

Here is the theory that I have come up with over the years. There was an Exodus undertaken by the Jews in the time the Bible speaks of. The Babylonians conquered Cain 'in and as it was customary of the day the inhabitants of the conquered country were taken back to the capital. Not necessarily for slavery but to assimilate them into society. After a lengthy and costly war with Egypt the Babylonians withdrew from Cain 'in and released the Jews to return to their home lands. We know that there were thousands of them; we also know that the event took place. I propose the possibility that the Exodus that the Bible is referring to is this journey from Babylon, and not Egypt.

There is the recorded history of the Jewish persecution by the Romans. The fact that the Romans were fought constantly, and were the victims of countless terrorist attacks, is something that the average Christian doesn't want to hear. What about the fact that the Christians slaughtered Muslims, Romans, and every other group of people that failed to bow to their God? I believe that the Romans treated the Jews as the Jews treated them; the reason we aren't taught this is because the Jews out lasted the Romans and they get to tell the story however they choose. Most Christians like to think they have been the victims, when in reality they were no better than the people that supposedly victimized them.

Now just to be fair; I must point out the fact that many countries, nations, and kingdoms of all sorts of religions have all committed atrocities against their fellow man. In fact I don't think there are any cultures that have distinguished themselves as being the morally good culture of history. I tend to pick on Christianity because they are the only ones that seem to think that their hands are clean. Maybe after they wash the blood from their eyes, they will truly be able to see.

The atrocity of the masses isn't where it all ends. There is the continuous manipulation of facts and opinions and politics. Religion has found its way into every facet of life; whether we want it or not. Again, I will focus on the Christians because of the fact that they above all others are consumed with converting, controlling, and oppressing others and their beliefs. In a class on ethics that I took the question was posed: If god asked you to kill your son, would you do it? In the Bible, God asked

Abraham to kill his son, was the reference. The answers that I heard were as amazing as they were terrifying. The one young man said: "If God told you to do it, how could you refuse?" Another said that they didn't believe that God would ever do such a thing. Yet there it is, in the writings of the Bible that you profess to be the book of your God.

The political part of the Bible started with the creation of the Roman Catholic Church. This has got to be the biggest contradiction that I have ever heard of. I grew up attending Sunday school, learning how the Romans tried to destroy the Jews and opposed Christianity. Rome became the Church, they are the Church, and when the Papal State was created and Christianity created their own government, the world would be changed forever. From that point, wholesale slaughter would be decided by the church, instead of warlords. Death would come in the name of salvation instead of conquest. In either case the dead are dead. Just because you change the name of it doesn't make it righteous.

The apocalypse, hell, and the end of days is fittingly the last subject that I want to analyze. Dante envisioned hell as a multiple level hotel of pain. Is hell really pain? According to the Bible there is only one place that refers to hell as a fiery pit. When God cast Lucifer out of Heaven, he is cast into a pit of fire and brimstone. All the other places in the Bible that talk about hell, it is described as a place of suffering, dark, and to live without the light of God, or the presence of god. In fact there is very little in the way of descriptive examples of hell in the Bible.

Biblically speaking hell has been interpreted as a blazing pit of fire because, we have a fundamental fear of fire. It is a classic fear response, nothing more. To many cultures hell could mean: a land without food, a land without people, or a land with no light or heat. Hell has been depicted in about every way imaginable. Hell for the Vikings is described as condemnation to the underworld and for those that were good, they would be released to Midgard, or middle earth, or more accurately: here. For the Greeks it was Hades, and there have been as many descriptions as there have been ideas. Some say that hell is to live without the presence of god. If that is true then I have been in hell from birth.

Most of the fire and brimstone concept that we have of hell is actually derived from Dante, a fictional book. My grandmother who was an incredibly religious person actually told me once that god would not allow people to go to hell. Hell was only meant for the unfaithful and it did not exist. She believed all people were good and in the end would go to heaven. Right or wrong, she truly believed in the concept that all people were good.

If I were to bear my soul then I would say, "To hell with me." I am a person with many things to regret, yet I do not. I have seen and done things that are not pleasant: I have fought and hurt, angered and killed, but I am not sorry, and never will be. If hell, in whatever form, is waiting for me then bring it on. I fear nothing, I regret nothing, and if I am to pay for eternity for something that I have done then; it only makes sense that I be proud of what I have done.

Hell is a metaphorical description of analogy, fear, and pain. Who wouldn't want to avoid that? Unfortunately the Bible isn't real clear on the whole process. It describes the role of St. Peter and the Pearly Gates. How on the Day of Judgment he will read from the book of life. Those whose names are not found in the book will not be granted entrance to Heaven. It's like a pot smoker's only club. And what is this book of life? If one can enter Heaven by repenting, why can't we just get there and say we are sorry, or has it all be decided already? According to one reading of the ancient texts, it is proscribed that hell is necessary, because if people think that they can achieve enlightenment, and there was no hell. Then what?

The concept of right and wrong is a subjective and sometimes controversial subject. The idea of hell is just an example of that control factor that allows people to justify their inability to punish those who deserve it, and condemn those who don't. We can't kill a convicted criminal because of humanitarian reasons. "It will be OK because they will pay for it in the next life." Sounds to me as if people are just not willing to take responsibility; it's always easier to just take a neutral position. What if St. Peter tells you that you will have to wait while the boss checks your file?

If you read and believe the Bible in its literal sense the world that we live in is hell. In Revelations there is a description of the Earth in the days in the end. Those days are called Armageddon, the Apocalypse, the Second Coming; all fantastical words that mean nothing. Seven seals, seven cities, four horsemen, and a thousand years of peace. Revelations speaks of many things of doom. It also talks of peace, for after the Anti Christ comes we will welcome him with open arms, and he will bring seven years of world peace. All we have to do to prevent the end of the world is reject world peace.

In the word of my favorite band (Man O War) "Armageddon, the first trumpet blows, hail fire and blood; by the morning sun the four horsemen ride." Har Megiddo (The hill of Megiddo) is the place, the Apocalypse is the unveiling, and the final battle is just a metaphor. The sun will turn black and the moon turn red, the dead will walk, the seas will die; all terrifying by themselves. It also talks about real things, such as an army of 200 million. No coalition or country can raise such a force, even briefly. An army of 200 million would equal 20 percent of the population of the largest country in the world; China. Plausible; yes; probable no: Especially if we expect seven years of peace before that.

Seven years of world peace; what a wonderfully ridiculous concept? It is a wonderful concept, on the surface, but unfortunately not very believable. On the other hand, once we achieve world peace, god plans on rewarding us with death and destruction. We will ultimately be rewarded by being allowed to serve god in his kingdom in the heavens. Again our reward for our suffering will be an eternity of servitude, which is just a nice word for slavery. At least in hell we will be free, if you look at it from a certain point of view.

Virtually every culture has had some version of hell and the end of the world. Now that many of those cultures have gone the way of the dinosaur, what are we to discern from the fact that their heaven and hell ceased to exist when they ceased to exist. Will Christian's heaven go away when they go away? If there is no one there to believe in it; does it exist at all, or did it ever exist? Culture, societies, countries, nations, and whole peoples have come and gone that never heard of Jesus Christ. Did they go to Heaven or Hell? What if you believe in a different god: do you go to Hell for that as well? What about the people that have never heard of Christianity, do they go to Heaven or Hell? Maybe it's a special club where only the truly special people get to play.

I think it would be downright embarrassing to die and find out that the Vikings had it right all the time. Or what if the Egyptians, Romans, or Greeks were the ones that had the "real" gods? I personally think it would be hilarious if the average Christian got to the Pearly Gates and there stood Thor with a mug of Mead, and with a big burly voice tells them that they weren't invited. Yes this is ridiculous, but that is what I think about the whole subject.

If I am to believe in the teachings of a mythical person, based entirely on the promise of eternal bliss, then they are going to have to try harder. Statistically speaking the Bible is the number one selling book of all time. Think about that logically for a minute. With more than 300 thousand hotels, motels, and inn's in this country alone: all of which have a Bible in every room, to say nothing of the fact that every soldier is issued a Bible, and every courthouse and jail have Bibles. It's pretty hard to convince me that it is the bestselling book because anyone bought it, or because anyone cares. My next point is a little subjective, but true; Hitler's book Mien Kampf is the second bestselling book of all time: just something to think about. There are many people that have gotten upset with this comparison, so don't think you're the first. I hate Hitler as much as anyone else, but I don't really care for the Bible that much either.

At the beginning of the chapter I explained why I am a non-believer and my problems with religion. As I stated earlier; I have the utmost respect for those who have the will and the fortitude to be a believer and I am not trying to convince anyone to change their opinions. My intention is and will always be to explain my opinion and defend my right to have that opinion. I will not bow, nor will I conform to any blind faith, because "I have none." Faith is hope, hope is dreams, and dreams are the subconscious ramblings of our mind.

I believe in hope. We all need hope, and dreams, but not one has ever been achieved because of faith. All of the dreams that have come true have been accomplished by hard work, dedication, and sacrifice. I have watched too many people in my life who thought that god would save them or god would get that job for them, or just believed everything would be fine if they had faith: suffer. Bad things happen, and there is nothing that can change that. There are good things that happen; I say accept them for what they are.

I believe very strongly in the morals of the Bible, but I believe in the values and morals of commonsense as well. I personally do not need a special book to threaten me to stop me from doing something that is wrong, nor do I need that same book to tell me when something is right. If an evil act is required to prevent an evil act and I am the one to stop it: rest assured that I will do what I must, and will gladly accept the consequences. If that means going to hell for my actions, then I say "see you in hell my friend."

Chapter 9

War

Any coward can turn the other cheek.
It takes courage to face a threat.
The will to survive, the vision to avoid the fight, when possible;
Is a triumph!
To fight without courage or will;
There is no vision!
To fight with courage and will without the vision to see victory;
Is a waste...

Men fight for three things:
Revenge; the one true passion
For pay; it is what we want most
For the Gods;
Because when all else fails we need something to believe in.

War what an ugly word: A word so dark and terrible that even politicians are afraid to say it. Now I agree that it is a word that I would rather not hear politicians talking about, but having been a soldier it is a word that I understand. I will try to leave the political views out of this chapter and concentrate on logic, and personal views of some of our rights and wrongs. This chapter will also be full of history and emotion. War is the one thing that creates strong emotions in me that I hide from people at most times. My emotions are something that I bury deep and only show certain people, but be prepared I will take you to the heart of darkness.

In this chapter I will take you to the gates of hell, but I will also try to bring you back before depression get the better of you. I will start with one of the greatest stories of self sacrifice in history. The last stand of the Spartan 300 is a true story of real people, and real courage, and so real that we are still telling the story 2500 years later.

What will you do that will be remembered for the ages? What have you ever done that will be talked about for centuries to come? How will you be remembered? Will you be remembered at all? If you are to be remembered, is it really that horrifying to be remembered for courage and sacrifice? Is it really so bad to be associated with something larger than yourself?

History tells the story, as written by Herodotus of a group of men that understood such questions. In 480 BCE Leonidus and his 300 Spartans would make their last stand at the pass of Thermopylae, and their names and deeds would be etched into stone and into history. Today at the site of the battle, there is a statue of Leonidus and below the inscription reads: **Ω ΞΕΙΝ ΑΓΓΕΛΛΕΙΝ ΛΑΚΕΔΑΙΜΟΝΙΟΙΣ ΟΤΙ ΤΗΔΕ ΚΕΙΜΕΘΑ ΤΟΙΣ ΚΕΙΝΩΝ ΡΗΜΑΣΙ ΠΕΙΘΟΜΕΝΟΙ** *"Go tell the Spartans passerby, that here obedient to their laws we lie."* What will they inscribe on your tomb?

The story of the 300 Spartans actually started ten years earlier in 490 BCE at the battle of Marathon. The Persians vowing revenge for the Greeks intervention in the invasion of Ionia set out with 600 ships loaded with Infantry, Calvary, and archers equaling 30 to 50 thousand troops. The Persians landed on the Greek coast and were met by 10,000 Hoplites from Greece on the plains of Marathon, about 26 miles north of Athens. Despite the fact that they were outnumbered, Miltiades, one of the Greek Generals decided to stand and fight. The Persians had a numerical advantage and their Calvary was the backbone of their army. The Hoplites on the other hand had the Phalanx, which loosely translated means forest of spears. The Phalanx is the one weakness that Calvary has. The Greeks were victorious. As the legend goes a messenger was sent by Miltiades to Athens to inform them of the victory. This messenger ran nonstop for twenty six miles and that is where we get the word Marathon that we use today originated. The runner informed the Greeks, and then died. This victory would not go un-noticed.

Darius was defeated at Marathon, but his son Xerxes was infuriated and vowed revenge. In 480 BCE he raised one of the largest fighting forces ever assembled and set his sights on Greece. Herodotus wrote that the army was over 2 million strong; most contemporary historians believe it was closer to 200 thousand. In either case it was a large army. Leonidus was the King of the Spartan City State of Greece. The Spartans had been used as the primary military force of Greece for centuries, because of their military capabilities. The Spartans trained from birth to be soldiers, and all Spartan males served in the military. No exceptions. It was entirely possible to have three, or even four or five generations of fathers and sons serving side by side in the Spartan military. This made them a fierce fighting force, one that would not be matched for centuries to come.

The Greek High Council felt that there was no way to win this battle and voted to retreat and surrender. Leonidus and the Spartans protested, but were forbid to interfere. Leonidus had a personal body guard of 300 soldiers, and in defiance of the councils wishes took them out on a training/reconnaissance mission. While doing so he sent word to several of the other Greek City States such as the, Arcadians, Corinthians, and several others to send aid and all the troops they could spare. In the meantime a man by the name of Damiticlies was attempting to build a naval force to cut off the Persians.

The Spartans knowing that they were horribly outnumbered knew that they had to create an advantage for themselves or all was lost. This advantage presented itself in the form of terrain. The pass at Thermopylae was a narrow pass about 75 feet wide with the sea to one side and a sheer cliff face to the other. That was where the Spartans would meet the Persians.

For three days they held the line. The rest of the army was getting weary and were taking heavy casualties. On the night of the second day Leonidus told the leaders of the other Greek states that if they wished to withdraw, no honor would be lost and thanked them for their service. They all left. The Spartans did not.

On the morning of the final day one of Xerxes messengers who were sent to ask for the Spartan surrender witnessed them bathing and polishing their armor. Mistaking this as a sign that they were going to withdraw the messenger returned to the Persian camp and reported what he had seen. Xerses was not satisfied with this and demanded that they surrender. The messenger returned to the Spartans. The messenger informed them that his lord Xerxes in honor of their bravery would let them live if they surrendered. The Spartans full heartedly refused. Then according to Herodotus the messenger said: *"If you do not surrender, we will blacken the skies with arrows."* The Spartans replied, *"Then we will fight in the dark."*

The final battle ensued, and at the end of the day every last Spartan lay dead on the field of battle. The messenger had mistaken their action that morning for them being ready to retreat. They were in fact preparing for their funerals. For the Spartans it was important to go to the afterlife looking the best that one could. To die in battle was the highest reward, and the greatest honor a Spartan could hope for.

With the Spartans defeated Xerxes marched on to Athens. When he arrived, he found the city abandoned. Against all odds and even on to death, Leonidus had succeeded. The inhabitants of Athens had time to evacuate leaving the city empty. In an eruption of anger Xerxes ordered the city raised to the ground. The following morning after realizing what he had done ordered it rebuilt. Xerxes would not however control it long enough to see this completed. In September of that same year Damiticlies came through and the Persians were defeated at the battle of Salamis. Xerxes limped home without his victory and the Persians never tried to invade Greece again.

Great deeds preformed by great men in terrible times. That is the lesson of the Spartan 300. Yes great deeds. The act of self sacrifice to save the lives of others is a great deed. Some may say that they could have retreated and negotiated, but history would have probably turned out completely different. Many historians believe that the story you just read was the defining moment in the development of western culture. Had the Persians won the whole world as we know it may be Muslim? Other Muslims would come and some would win a few battles and even a few wars, but none as pinnacle as Thermopolis.

I feel that the Spartans understood something that we have long forgotten. Service to the greater good and sacrifice for what is right are great deeds. To fight and die in defense of one's land or country is the highest honor a person can achieve, with the exception of fighting and surviving. For the soldier war isn't about choices, war is about duty. We stand and fight for those who will not or cannot. We pay for the freedom that you spend, we are the consequences of your choices, but at least I did it with pride. The least people could do is remember who we are and what we have done for the people of this country.

There are some common themes that I will follow in this chapter.

First; there is the need of the many to be thankful of the few. Second; there is the need of the few to realize that the lives of the many are more important than that of the few. Last; all need to realize that freedom is not paid for in dollars, GDP's, the DOW, or politicians. Freedom is paid in blood; the blood of those willing to give and spill it. I read a bumper sticker once that read: *"If you can read this; thank a teacher. If you can read this in English, thank a soldier."* This sums up my opinion on American history pretty well.

War is a terrible thing to comprehend. Yet this country would not exist if it wasn't for war. In fact if we were to just sit back and have done nothing, I would surmise that the American map would look very different, if this country existed at all.

Sometimes it is easy to think that those deeds of the past are but deeds of the past: The distant past. These are not all ancient deeds done buy ancient people. These are deeds and actions taken every day by people that you know. Some would say; "That is different." I would agree that war today is different; in its design, its politics, and even its reasons. What isn't different is the fact that people, or more accurately young people that believe in something greater than themselves; agree to put their lives on the line for you. Throughout history there are the billions of lives given for some country, state, town, or cause that are pitched to the wind every time someone protests a war.

Protest is freedom of speech and I fully support the fact that people have the right to voice their opinion. However that is something that we must remember. Protest is not change; it is just opinion and has never really led to any real change. I just wish that people would learn to voice their opinions before we have dead soldiers on the battle fields of the world. Simply put: Make up your mind before we go. As a soldier there is nothing that makes me angrier then when people support the war then they don't support the war, then they don't know why we went, then finally it is wrong somehow, and we should have never done it. There are no do-over's on the battle field.

When they landed on Normandy they didn't get to say; OH MY, this is worse than we thought. Can we try this a different way? The American people think that war is like video games were if your favorite character dies you just start over. In my opinion, there is nothing to be protested, after it starts.

As I already said war is a terrible thing. There are however times and places that it is the only choice. I have heard all the arguments.

Some of my favorite include: Violence only brings violence. If that were true then why are we not at war with England, Germany, Japan, Spain, Mexico, Puerto Rico, the Philippines, or the Native Americans? These are all countries that we have been at war with in the past. Then there is the ever popular: Violence doesn't solve anything. Not unless you wish to be free from oppression, slavery, genocide, or wish to obtain a free country: All of which have been won and paid for with blood. You don't really think that any of these things were ever achieved from talking nicely??? In fact this brings me to a thought. The only countries that we still have major problems with that we have been at war with are the two in which we were not allowed by the American people to win. Namely: Korea and Vietnam. Hell even Qadhafi wants to be our friend and we killed half of his family.

It's not my intention to make this chapter a history lesson, but I will use history were it is necessary, and useful to make a point. At this point I would like to introduce you to one of my childhood heroes. Yes I had many but Sgt. Alvin C. York was one of them. Believe it or not yes; Sgt. York was a childhood hero. Sgt. York was an uneducated and devoutly religious man who found himself in a world of death. He applied for conscientious objector status and was denied, after being drafted in 1917. He believed that war was wrong, killing was wrong, and fighting someone that you didn't even know was wrong. After all how can you hate someone bad enough to go to war with them if you don't even know them?

With time he distinguished himself as an expert marksman, and was diligently honest. Still he opposed the war, and even if forced to go he vowed not to fight. After much coercion from his commander he realized that he had no choice but to go. He relented and gave up his protest and was sent to France. While in the Meuse-Argonne he found himself and sixteen of his comrades lost and behind enemy line. As fate would have it they discovered that they were surrounded, outnumbered, and had no idea which way to the friendly lines.

It was about this time that the enemy realized that they had intruders. The German machine guns opened up and started to cut down York's friends. While this was going he remembered something that his commander said: If a good man allows another man to be killed, is he not as guilty as the man doing harm? In the fray Sgt. York made his choice. One by one the machineguns fell silent through York's sights.

York and his companions went on to capture over a hundred German soldiers and officers.

Sgt. York was awarded the Congressional Medal of Honor for his actions in the Argonne. He eventually returned home and was sent on a bond selling tour. He would recount his story as necessary for the crowds, but never admitted that he was a hero. In his humble way he simply explained that he did what he had to do, and that God would ultimately decide if it was right. In the end the lives of his friends and comrades won the argument.

It's my view that Sgt. York learned that sometimes the worst choice is still the right choice, or at least the best under the circumstances. If we are to understand the terrible choices that soldiers all over the world face we need to face those questions ourselves. To paraphrase what Emanuel Kant once wrote: if war is the answer then we should commit to it with all our vigor so as to have it done. A famous quote states: *"No one hates war more than the warrior, for he shall bare the deepest of wounds."* Sun Tzu wrote that *"he who can win without loss of life is the true victor."* He wasn't necessarily talking about the enemy. Sgt. York was not the last to make this realization.

There have been many others, and some of them are in our midst yet today; many are not. People such as Col. Greg "Pappy" Boyington, Gen. George S. Patton, were in my opinion visionary in their resolve, and their commitment to win. Another one of my heroes was Sir Winston Churchill. I always respected him because he was a great leader, speaker, and person, yet he made some of the most horrible choices that we can imagine. I have always found inspiration in his words, such as what he spoke after Dunkirk: *"Never before in the annals' of history have so many owed so much too so few."* Or when he referred to the battle of England as: England's finest hour. This was a man that understood what was necessary to win, to fight, and to die for.

Unlike the wars of history there really aren't any conquerors anymore. The days of Ghangius Khan, Attila the Hun, Alexander the Great, or Ramses IV are truly gone. Likely for most we only try to conquer through economic means today. No; the wars of today are fought in different ways with different goals. Even as the goals are different, so too are the methods required to impede those advances. If you believe the movies a good negotiator can talk people into doing anything. I don't believe the movies.

Look at World War II. How many Nazi's did we kill? What did we kill them for? Many people will argue that is different because they were committing genocide against the Jews. The only problem is; we didn't really know that until the end of the war. What were we fighting for in the mean time? We were fighting against unbridled aggression against a free state. We fought the Japanese because they invaded Manchuria, and they attacked us. We went to war with Germany because they were attacking our allies. There is much more to it than that but I have already discussed much of that.

We fought in World War I because President Wilson thought it necessary for us to become a world power. We fought World War II much for the same reason. Then there was Korea. We fought there because we feared communism, and they asked us for help. Vietnam was the same. In my life I have watched the invasion of Granada, and Beirut, and Panama. I lived through Desert Storm, Mogadishu Somalia, and Bosnia. After Desert Storm we all knew that we (The U.S.) were going back. We left unfinished business. I have spent thirty five years of my life watching flag draped coffins unloaded from planes. If I never see one again it will be too soon. At the same time I would rather see ten thousand then watch the genocide of Kosovo or Darfur. Maybe I should do like most and just not pay attention or watch the news. It is much easier to bury our heads in the sand. To do anything else would undoubtedly, upset someone.

The reasons we fight are numerous and complex. How we fight can be as confusing. In ages past armies would assemble at a predetermined area, form up, and then fight until one or the other gave in. It was bloody, violent, and savage, but it was civilized to a degree. Many times entire wars could be decided with one battle. When the Normans invaded England under William the Conqueror in 1066, there were only the two major battles. The Battle of Stamford Bridge, and a few days later at the Battle of Hastings, the war was over. Then of course there are the Crusades, and the Hundred Year war, but neither were wars that actually went on for hundreds of years. They were both just a series of wars the history has a hard time telling were one ended and the next began.

Today we have technology, intelligence, equipment and manpower that the ancients could only dream of. Yet we have been fighting an ill-equipped unorganized group of idiots, following a group of fanatics bent on the destruction of the United States. Words like insurgency,

IED (Improvised Explosive Device) are words that the modern media think that they dreamt up. Guerilla warfare, search and destroy, and calculated strikes, are things that were dreamt up in the 20th century. Wrong!

In some ways wars are fought the same today as they were thousands of years ago. They are fought with people, armor, tactics, and whatever means necessary for victory. Terrorism is just one of those words. In all of the American wars we have used terrorism, piracy, and insurgency to fight those who we opposed.

In the modern war there have come many questions of ethics. The use of torture is just one of these questions. According to the Geneva Convention the use of torture is forbidden. This of course depends on the interpretation of the law as to what torture is. According to several dictionaries I referred to: Torture is defined as follows: *"To cause or inflict sever pain."* (Webster's, Scott Foresman and Company Advanced Dictionary, as well as a couple of on-line dictionaries) So when discussing water boarding you simply have to ask yourself if it fits the definition. Whether you like the definition or not it is not torture: and therefore not against the law. As a friend of mine said; "It doesn't matter what we call it is still wrong." That may or may not be true, but the point is whether it is legal or not. People have to remember that a personal opinion does not make it law. I would personally be OK with whatever methods that were required to get the information needed. They are the enemy after all.

This brings me to another good argument. Which are the terror trials of the Christmas day bomber, Umar Farouk Abdulmutallab, and the now infamous Ft. Hood Massacre allegedly perpetrated by Maj. Nidal Malik Hasan. The question/argument over whether they deserve a fair trial in a Federal Court, or if they deserve to be tried in a military court has become another one of the debates, that in my opinion there is nothing to discuss. The predominant question is whether or not they are combatants. The law in my mind is pretty clear. If they are combatants, then the military has jurisdiction, if they are not the Federal Courts have the jurisdiction. Again I hate to reduce such a heated and opinionated argument down to simple terms taken from the average dictionary, but I have no choice. The law, as well as Webster's Dictionary, and other sources all agree that the definition of a combatant is as follows: *"Someone that takes part in the fight, or combat:*

Someone that actively supports by action that of combat – To participate in the act of aggression against an enemy power or nation."

I wish to point out that in these definitions there is no mention as to the reasons for which they chose to act; just the fact that they did. There is also no mention as to whether they we ordered or recruited to do such action. Just the fact that they acted in support of one or the other combative nations involved. Last there is no mention of the person or person's involvement in these actions about their mental state or capability.

We have two separate instances with two different people in different circumstances. So I will start with Maj. Nidal Malik Hasan, and the Ft. Hood Massacre. For a person to premeditatedly arm themselves, and go to a predetermined location, and scream "Allahu Ahkbar before opening fire and killing 13 American troops and civilians and wounding 30 more is in my opinion the act of a extremist. A radical extremist; acting the interest of his faith, and his peoples struggle against the United States, to cause destruction, death, and terror. So the question is whether he is a combatant, or not. One only need to look at the definition and ask themselves: Did he participate in an act of aggression in the name of an enemy faction in which we are presently at war with?

My opinion is probably obvious, but whether you agree or not the law states that the crime was committed on military soil, against military personnel, therefore it is a military matter. Then there is the accusation of Hasan suffering from PTSD: Ridiculous, since he has never served in combat. Then there is the argument that he was a disturbed and troubled man. Most mass murderers are, but what does that change? Nothing! Last there are the accusations that he simply feared being deployed. If that were true then he is guilty of treason and therefore a military matter and well within their jurisdiction. Regardless this appears to be a military matter and not a civilian one.

Now let's analyze the Christmas Day bomber or should I say the attempted underwear bomber. Umar Farouk Abdulmutallab, focused his efforts on a civilian target, but was trained in Yemen by Al-Qaeda to undertake the mission. While acting in their charge he became a combatant the minute he agreed to carry out the attack. Again according to the dictionary he was acting in the interest of an enemy that we are currently at war with. *According to the Geneva Conventions III Art-84 a prisoner of war shall only be tried by the military unless so authorized by the military.*

Last thing that I wish to touch on concerning this point is the fact that some have claimed that these people couldn't receive a fair trial in the military. This has been brought up in the case of Maj. Nidal Malik Hasan because of the fact that both the perpetrator and the victims were military. It has been surmised that the judges and other military personnel in the case would be especially sympathetic on behalf of the victims and he would be convicted either way. This is completely laughable to me.

There simply isn't any question as to whether or not he committed the crime. If Hasan can't receive a fair trial because of military sympathy, then what do we do with suspected police killers? The jury is made up of the people that they are supposed to protect, and the witnesses are all friends and co-workers, and last the judge probably knows the victim and his or her family. Is that a fair trial?

The lines in battle are not always clear and therefore the opinions and theories can get confused as well. In Vietnam, much like today the enemy used any and all resources available. That means using terrorism. The use of women and children as weapons are as old as war is. The use of insurgence to cause mayhem and destruction is as well. It is not surprising to me that people get confused about the rules of engagement and how to function in a battle. Most people have never done it and I hope none of you will ever have to. In combat soldiers have to make life and death decisions based only on their instincts! If they make the wrong choice someone dies.

This brings me to the next subject, and that is how does one fight a war where the battle lines aren't clear and even your enemy isn't necessarily what or who you think they are. Just how do you fight and/or defeat an enemy that looks and acts like everyone else. Like I said earlier in ancient times armies would meet on a field of battle and engage and when the battle was at its conclusion both sides walked away. After the Battle of Hastings in 1066 King William built an Alter on the exact sit where King Herald fell. Later still he had a church built to pay tribute to the fallen from both sides. Respect and honor of one's enemy is something that is hard for many to grasp.

War is many times depicted as a hateful act in which soldiers who hate their opponents are all too fiercely happy to kill their enemy. This may be true in some cases but it is not true in most. Soldiers are all too aware that their enemies are people. I have had this conversation and even this argument far too often. I was trained to kill Russians, and I can honestly say that I don't and have never hated or even disliked Russians. I have been asked to explain how is it possible to fight and kill someone that you respect. This is one of those places that for me the emotional side of this discussion inserts itself.

Soldiers don't hate their enemy; in fact many times we understand and respect them more than the people back home protesting the war. We have no reason to hate anyone; they just like us are just doing their job. Just doing our job: Sounds so dry and simple? Quite the contrary, there is nothing simple about it.

In war just as in peace, soldiers are charged with some of the greatest of tasks. Their "job" is to fight, defend, and sacrifice for those whom cannot. In the fight, it is their job to deprive the enemy of the will and/or capability to wage aggression. In defense they are charged with the task of responding to threats, where ever, when ever, and without regards for where the threat comes from. With duty and sacrifice they achieve these tasks. Throughout all this they are trained to make choices. Many times that job description includes the taking of a life. Soldiers have many burdens to bear and in one way or another we all have our demons.

My demons don't have faces or names, and there is very little to describe. They are shapes in the dark, and to be honest I don't really know that anyone died. Maybe I just prefer it that way, but it is true. The only face and name that I know was my first. He was my best friend. I shot him in a hunting accident, too stupid and too complicated to explain. What I can say is that even twenty five plus years later, I still wake up in the night and hear the words: "I'm hit."

This is not the case for at least my one friend. He watched his first kill up close and personal in every disgusting detail through the scope of his sniper rifle. Others still such as the one friend that was Navy SEAL had several stories that would be too much to hear for some. No one can explain that which someone else has not done. All I can say about that is that there are times when life, fate, or the world places you in a place and a time, with a choice. I won't discuss my choices, but I will say that I am OK with them. I am here, I have my friends and my wife, I have life and my dogs, and that is because of the choices I made. So do I respect my enemies? Yes with all my heart. They were people, with families and friends, and hopefully fighting for something they believe in.

In times of war soldiers are not asked whether they want to fight or if the war is the right thing to do or not. Like the old saying: *"It is not for us to wonder why, it is but for us to do and die."* Plato wrote: *"Only the dead have seen the end of war."* Aristotle said: *"We make war so we may live in peace."* Ironically Hitler once said; *"The victor will never be asked if they were wrong."* Different perspectives yet all true from a certain point of view. The fact is soldiers are a necessary evil. An evil that I am proud to have been part of! If it was necessary and I was in the situation I would still give my life to defend those that hate people like me. That is what makes me a soldier.

I promised that I would not make this political, and I did not lie. I do however feel that I need to point out one important fact. I cannot say this is true for other soldiers or anyone for that matter, but when asked about whether I agree with the war in Iraq or Afghanistan, I am honestly forced to answer: "I have no idea." The fact is that the war is going on; the time to decide whether it is right or wrong is long past. In this I fully agree with Gen. Douglas MacArthur when he said; *"it is fatal to enter into any war without the will to win it."* That is what we need to be talking about; "Winning the dam thing."

The first thing we need to do is get rid of the bleeding heart attitude. War is terrible, horrible, and deadly; I knew that; as have every soldier that ever signed on the dotted line. The best way to honor them and honor their families is to make it worth it. To this end I say "unleash the hounds." In my opinion there is only one quick way to bring a war to an end. Let the people that are trained to do this, do this. We need to disregard the politics and the politicians all together. Don't get me wrong I believe in the just war concept and in part it states that a war should only be authorized by the appropriate power. Once however the decision has been made get out of the way and let us make it end.

If I were Commander and Chief (Assuming Congress already approved) I would assemble my war room and my Generals and give them a simple task. I want this war over in one year (For example), tell me what you need: you have one week, no get to work and get me that list. Emanuel Kant wrote, the just war concept, but he also wrote: *"Do what is right, though the world may perish."* I am also a fan of Winston Churchill, he had many great speeches, but the one that I think of in this scenario is when he said: *"The whole history of the world can be summed up in the fact that, when nations are strong they are not always just, when they wish to be just they are no longer strong."*

Now as much as I admire Lord Churchill, I must say that I do disagree with him on this point at least a little. I feel that a nation must focus on being just at least when at peace, however when war shows its ugly face then lets attack it with all we have.

When should we go to war? It is easy to sit back and say never. It is easy to believe that there is always another way to get our way. Let's be clear; that is what war is about most of the time. We were attacked at Pearl Harbor in 1941 not because the Japanese were evil warmongers. We got attacked because we were trying to stop the war in Manchuria. In other words we stuck our nose into other people business. We could argue all day about whether they were right or wrong for their aggression against Manchuria, but either way it was still their business, not ours. So again I ask what makes it appropriate to go to war.

The bottom line is; I don't know when it is the right thing or when it is wrong. I know it is wrong to idly stand by while other people are suffering. I know it is wrong to turn our back on those who can't defend themselves. I know it is wrong to allow governments to oppress, and kill their own people in the name of racial purity. Most of you would hopefully agree that all these acts are wrong.

So we need to ask ourselves when has it gone too far, and what do we do when politics and sanctions don't work. I have heard far too many people talk about how this or that is wrong, but are really willing to do nothing about it. I had a couple of friends that served in Bosnia and all I can say about that is the disgust that they felt at the fact that they couldn't do anything. In the eighty's when the Marine barracks in Beirut was destroyed and 263 Americans died because of politics, I knew that to stand by and let atrocities happen and do nothing makes you just as bad as the perpetrators.

Protesting and sanctioning and imposing United Nations support is the same as doing nothing if they fail. In my opinion it is the same as when somebody goes to a bad neighborhood and end up getting killed. There are some that would say "I told them they shouldn't go." They probably think they did everything they could. I quote what Stalin once said when he stated: *the death of one man is a tragedy; the death of a million is a statistic.* This sounds absolutely horrifying, yet that is exactly how we react in these situations. We protest, and beg our governments to do something, and when they do and it is unsuccessful we will blame them for not trying hard enough. We will say we are doing all we can. In the meantime thousands are dying at the hands of a dictator or some other monster. Sometimes the death of thousand to save millions is just the best way to stop the madness. Maybe madness is just the best way to defeat insanity.

In the words of Shakespeare: (Julius Caesar Act II scene II) *"Cowards die many times before their deaths; the valiant never taste of death but once. Of all the wonders that I yet heard it seems to me most strange that men should fear; seeing that death, a necessary end, will come when it comes."* If I never see a flag draped coffin again it will be too soon. If I must I only hope that it can be in the service of our country and in the service of those who can't fight for themselves. I would rather bleed on foreign soil to prevent the blood from being spilled on ours.

In WWI many people were convinced that they were fighting the war to end all wars. Upon completing this noble task the world would be able to live in peace. What I find so compelling about this idea is the fact that so many people actually believed it. They honestly thought that there would never be another war. Ironically there are people from our own time that have the same disillusioned ideals. Like during the Clinton years when we had some of the largest military cuts in history. This opened the door for 9/11 and I feel they are just as much to blame as Bin laden. I fear that one day war will come to our land, and all of these optimistic well wishers will be faced with an enemy that cannot be reasoned with. Maybe when the day comes that we are powerless to choose if or when we fight people will learn the value of vigilance, and preparedness. If any country is to enjoy peace then they must be prepared for war.

"You have enemies?
Good, that means that you have stood up for something,
sometime in your life."
(Lord Winston Churchill)

"The further back we look
The farther forward we are likely to see."
(Lord Winston Churchill)

"We're at war dam it! We shall have to offend someone."
(John Adams)

Chapter 10

Myth and Legend

Just because science won't accept it doesn't mean it's not factual.
With history as the example: The more they don't believe
it the more likely it will turn out to be true.
The definition of science is: Knowledge based on <u>observed</u> facts
and tested truths arranged in an orderly system. (Webster's)
Even the definition flies in the face of mainstream science.
Apparently they only trust their own observations.

Where would we be if our imagination and our fear of the unknown had not forced us to the brink of discovery? What if some of those fears could be proven? The world is full of wonders and discoveries yet to be hold. Many of the things I address in this chapter will be fantastical, and even unbelievable. I wish only to state my opinion and bring theories to the mysteries that I will examine in this chapter. There are many things that were once thought to be legend, but were then proven to be true.

The Giant Panda was considered to be a myth until the late 50's, and the Coelacanth was believed to be extinct for 70 million years. Both are real and have been studied at length. Even the Komodo dragon was considered to be a myth, but here they are. Then as recently as 2006 a large new species of ape was discovered in Africa. First photographed by Shelly Williams, (Primatologist) these apes have been reported by locals for decades but have been written off by the large mainstream science community. Even with all this denial, the apes still exist.

The question has come to mind; why should I take such a serious, opinionated, and analytical way of approaching this book, just to cloud it with mysterious conjecture about myths and legends. The fact is that I believe that the quest for discovery and knowledge is never wrong. Even if that means looking for Bigfoot! We would probably still believe that the world was flat if it wasn't for a group of individuals that decided to find out. Yes; that was centuries ago, but it still happens today. Rouge Waves were considered to be the tales of drunken sailor and poor Captaining, for decades if not centuries. Within the last twenty years they have not only been documented but they have been photographed and studied.

Twenty short years ago rouge waves were just a figment of people's imagination, yet they are big enough to be seen from space and can easily be tracked today. Many years ago I was watching a TV program about missing and lost ships, and there was the "Expert" that claimed that rouge waves were just impossible. To paraphrase, he actually said: "People actually expect us to believe that on a calm day without a storm or cloud in the ski, a wave just comes up and smashes the ship: Preposterous!" I for one would love to know what that guy is studying today.

The fact that something has not been proven to be true, and has not been accepted by science is hardly grounds for complacency, and conformity. The fact that so many people see, report, document, photograph, and are willing to undergo the ridicule of openly saying that they believe in them is proof to me that something profound happened. We have people in this world that are afraid to admit that they are gay, and at the same time we have people that believe in god. Both are accepted, and yet one is taboo, and the other is considered fact by many.

So yes I feel that the study and the investigation of these subjects are serious and important. I find it hard to believe that any real scientist would not jump at the chance to prove or disprove any of these phenomenons. They would argue that they only deal in facts. Let's look at that for a moment. In addition to that I wish to take an overly serious group of subjects and lighten the mood by talking about something that I just enjoy theorizing about.

Let us look at the facts. Photographs are too difficult to make out and get real evidence from. Photos can or are hoaxed or fake. My favorite is that they are not taken by professional photographers, who know how to get the best shot, and therefore most are blurry, out of focus, and there are no frames of reference. I could say the same thing about every surveillance camera ever used in a criminal investigation. Strangely enough when a good piece of footage comes along they instantaneously debunk it as a hoax because it is too good or because it looks professionally made. Kind of makes me wish they would make up their mind.

The next flawed factual evidence is the eyewitnesses themselves. Virtually every facet of our lives is in one way or another based on eyewitness interpretation. Our criminal system is based on eyewitnesses. Astronomy is based on observation. Reconnaissance and military intelligence is gathered and acted on through eyewitness observations. Picture if you will that you see a drug deal or a drunk driver and the police ask are you sure. Or they just discredit your report altogether because you're not a trained observer. Either people see what they see or we are all wrong, only one can be true. If we can trust people to condemn others to prison, then we must trust their ability to know when they have seen something fantastical.

My next argument goes alone with the last. That is the fact that many would assert that we don't necessarily condemn people based entirely on eyewitness reports. We use several correlating pieces of evidence and if they are all in agreement then there is a case. Evidence that just a few years ago is now being overturned left and right, because they were flawed and inaccurate. We use several forms of evidence to convict people. Some of these include forensics, phonological, and behavioral profiling, as well as things such as ballistics, and fingerprinting. However in addition to all of that we still use circumstantial and eyewitness testimony to convict. In many cases eyewitness reports are enough to bring an indictment and all of the scientific evince in the world can still fail to convict.

Out of the 2.3 million convicted prisoners' in the country, there are a large majority of them that got there because of eyewitness. In conclusion on the subject of eyewitnesses, I would surmise that there are more people that have seen Bigfoot than have seen god. While I was researching different things for this book I had a strange thought and decided to do some comparisons of people's beliefs on these types of subjects. What I discovered amazed me to say the least.

It turns out that people actually believe in the existence of Bigfoot and UFOs more than they believe in things such as evolution, the Big Bang, our government, and our legal system. According to an article written 12 February 2009 by Mark Murry for MSNBC, stated some amazing results. Surprisingly 58% of people believe in God, 35% in Evolution, 16% trust our legal system, and 34% trust our government as compared to: 58% believe in Bigfoot, 80% believe in UFOs. This lies in conjunction with the over 400,000 Bigfoot reported sightings and the more than 1000 per year sightings of UFOs.

If there were a competition between science, myth, and legend, the scientists are losing badly, and clearly not making their case very believable. I feel that if it is truly possible that all these people are wrong, in their beliefs and their sightings then we have a serious problem. A serious enough problem that should require scientific study and attention, verification of and/or against any of these subjects only lend themselves to knowledge and discovery.

The subject of Bigfoot evokes fear, speculation, skepticism, and disbelief. It also invokes emotional memories of what people experienced, seen or heard. For the skeptic it is easy to not believe. "I have never seen one, or why haven't we found a dead one?" The questions are many and for the skeptic the answer is simple. "They are not real, and people are just mistaken by what they see. For the witnesses and/or believers no explanation is good enough. I know this because I have seen things that I can't explain. The question that I ask myself is "what was that thing I saw?" "What could it be?" I have had five distinct sightings and another half dozen situations that involved something that was not right. In every case there were several mundane and unimaginative explanations, and when all others have been ruled out then the examination must be that you misinterpreted what you saw, or you were just making it up.

Near where I live there were reports of a Black Panther roaming the woods. Everyone treated this much the same as a Bigfoot sighting. It quickly became more of a joke than something of a mystery. The tracks were nothing more than misidentified coyote tracks and the sightings were explained by everything from some drunk said he saw to an old woman that probably saw a big tomcat. This went on for a couple years until a local rancher shot and killed the animal. They then discovered that there was not one, but six of them. The rest were captured and transferred to local zoos and the official explanation determined that they must have escaped from a zoo somewhere.

Regardless of the official explanation there were breeding group of Black Panthers living the local forest and through further investigation the local DNR concluded that they had been there for at least ten years. What no one was willing to explain was how a group of 250 pound cats could be living in a populated area for ten years and nobody know it. The DNR and the local hunters had no explanations. Ironically they were the ones that believe it all to be a hoax to begin with.

The point of this story is that this is not a great expanse of forest like the American North West or many other remote locations. It was a well populated popular hunting location with hundreds of people traveling these woods every year. Out of these hundreds of visitors and local hunters, and even the DNR, only a handful of sightings were ever reported. None of which were taken with any seriousness.

Another argument that I hear frequently is; how come we don't find dead bodies or other evidence. Where I grew up as a kid the local wildlife included deer, coyotes, wolves, and bear, all well documented and known to exist. With all my years of walking those woods I have never found the dead body of a wolf, bear, or any large mammal. In fact I very seldom ever found dead animals at all even little ones. I have on occasion found a deer, or a wild dog but they never lasted long either. When I asked a local Game Warden about the subject he simply told me that unless you come across the dead animal within a short period of time after its death you won't find remains. Mother Nature has a way of cleaning up after herself.

In reality I have never heard even one valid argument that proves that they don't exist. There have been simply too many sightings, footprints, hair samples, and nests that have been located to rule out the possibility of a large primate living around the world that is as yet not been documented. Now from my point of view that is exactly what we are talking about; a primate, not some mythical monster of legend.

What if: and this is just a proposal from the mind of a common person with common sense. What if they are just primates who evolved along a separate line? We know that humans and apes had a common ancestor in the ancient past. At some point the species diverged from one another, and still lived along side each other. Gigatopithecus lived side by side with our ancestors and were believed to die out around 200,000 years ago around the end of the Pleistocene era.

There are many things that we know exist that we thought to have died out much earlier than that. So what if they too continued to evolve separate from us? Perhaps they are much more intelligent than we think. We assume that our gismos and gadgets are what make us smart and prove our intelligence. What if they evolved and never embraced technology and invention, preferring to live as nature intended. We know from experience that if someone wants to not be found, it is possible to disappear all together. Hundreds of people do it every year. What if they are just smart enough to not be found? As a soldier I was trained to live off the land and to leave no trace of my presence. In my experience if something or someone doesn't want to be found it won't be found.

The most recent discoveries have indicated that Gigantopihecus lived as recent as 150 thousand years ago. Everything that we know about Gigantopithecus is derived from twelve separate fossils. Twelve pieces of evidence and from that we think we know how they lived and when they died. Twelve individual pieces of circumstantial evidence that wouldn't stand a chance in a court of law! When it comes to this kind of evidence science is just as guilty as the people they say are misidentifying the creatures.

Yes; I feel that the search for and study of Bigfoot is worthwhile. The discovery of just such a beast would or at least could be one of the most important anthropological discoveries of the millennium. The ultimate proof of evolution could lie in the discovery of Bigfoot. Maybe it is just another primate that wishes nothing but to be left alone in peace. Science will require one of them to die before they accept their existence; this proves how heartless and utterly insane science can be. This type of arrogant destructive sense of logic is exactly what has caused our society to fall into disillusion.

There are other mysteries in the world such as UFOs, and extra terrestrials, and the possibility that we have been visited in the past. Again this is a subject that I believe disserves more study by science. I have many mixed feelings about science but I believe they are good at studying things once you give it to them on a silver platter. For example the Giant Panda was a myth until somebody handed it over. Science is great at investigating things after they have them, apparently it is too difficult to go look. It would be easier if they just wait for someone else to do the work. That way they don't have to be wrong. So when it comes to investigating anything that is less than perfect, they will just sit back and wait for someone to drop in their lap.

UFOs are no different. I remember as a child someone making the comment that if these aliens are so smart why don't they just land on the Whitehouse lawn and say; "Hi, how's it going, can we be friends?" I love how simple minded some people can be. This would undoubtedly be simple for the aliens assuming that they wanted to be our friends, and they actually recognized the United States as being important. All we must do is look at ourselves to understand why they might not want to just open dialogue with us. When was the last time a scientist walked into the middle of a lion pride and asked if they could be friends, or if it would be OK to study them.

Before you criticize this opinion by telling me that they are just animals, I would have to point out: that is probably what an advanced species capable of interstellar travel would think of us. For all we know they think of about the same as we think of an ant colony.

Let's examine the theory that Erich Von Daniken proposed in his book "Chariots of the Gods". In his book as well as several documentaries about ancient aliens on the History channel, there have been some seriously commonsense evaluations of some of our ancient sites and mysteries. Why do pyramids for example, show up on several continents and all date from around the same period. There are several examples of megalithic structures and unexplained constructions all over the world. I refer to them as unexplained because I feel that science has failed to do them justice and explain anything.

I will start with one of my favorite mysteries, at Puma Punku and Tiahuanaco in Bolivia. The site has been dated to around 17,000 years old. That is 12,000 years older than the pyramids at Giza and 9,000 years older than the earliest writings on earth. Structures made from stones weighing over 100 tons with the largest at 440 ton and cut to perfection using only simple tools. I find this very hard to believe. If this type of megalithic structure came from trial and error, where are the failed structures, where are the ruins of these previous attempts? Maybe they reused the material; on the other hand the ruins at Puma Punku were not reused. Maybe they had help?

Structures of this nature could have been for many things, but the structure at Tiahuanaco and Puma Punku are very strange indeed. Who built them and for what reason? Where did everyone go and most importantly what event caused the structures to be left in ruins? Something that I have always found interesting about these particular ruins is the seemingly random destruction of the sight. Part of the sight is made up of perfectly fitted stones using nothing to hold them together. Other structures are made from these interlocking stones that are perfectly fitted as well. The interlocked stones were destroyed by some catastrophic force, while the fitted, but free standing structures are for the most part intact.

These sights are many and the mysteries only get more complicated. The Nazca Lines of Peru, Easter Island in the pacific, Avebury, Stonehenge in England, and the mystery of Atlantis, are all just such places that should be looked at with different eyes. Too many times I feel that just like in Egypt these scientists are so convinced with their correctness that even when a new discovery is made it is just formed to fit what they think they already know. What I feel happens in these cases such as with Puma Punku the evidence does not fall into their understanding of things so it must be false. Aliens fit this example to a tee.

Why is it so hard for science to accept the fact that we are and have been visited by intelligent life for perhaps several millennia? The answer is simple in my mind. Science can't stand the fact that there may be someone or something out there that is smarter and more advanced than we are. In the vastness of space and the billions of worlds that occupy that space I personally have no doubt that there are many species of more intelligence out there. The only argument that I have that would indirectly support the scientific community; why in the world would they care about us?

Out of all the mysteries in the world, UFOs have got to be the most likely to exist and the most likely to be proven. There are plenty of pieces of evidence to support that fact that we have been visited. Contrary to people's opinions such as Todd Disotell PHD of the University of New York who believes that it is simply not possible. Furthermore he asserts that no serious scientist should waste their time on these fantasies that have no evidence. (Taken from the History Channel program, Ancient Aliens.) I say it is hard to see evidence when your eyes are closed.

Other mysteries include: The Antikythera Mechanism, The Coso Artifact (Ancient Spark Plug), impossible fossils, (Including a 300 million year old human foot print) forged metal objects that are buried in stone hundreds of millions of years old, and even a human skull reportedly found on the Moon and one on Mars. Then there is the face on Mars and the apparent structure found in the place known a Sardonia. The face on Mars has over and over again been explained as a trick of light and shadow. The fact that there was a recent photo taken that makes it appear less like a face was very unimpressive to me. The fact that it appears weathered and aged and more like a mountain just tells me that it is ancient. I highly doubt that many of our structures will look the same in fifty thousand years. Even the faces on Mt. Rushmore will probably not look much like people in a hundred thousand years.

Life on Mars: Could it be that is where we came from? We know that there was an atmosphere and water on the surface at one time. Maybe we will discover that the inhabitants destroyed their world and moved on. Now we are trying to do it again. I believe that it would be incredible poetic to discover that we and the Martians are actually one in the same. Is it really that bizarre to think that we actually came from somewhere else? If we believe Darwin we lived here for millions of years and suddenly learned how to make tools, talk, build things, and then to build big megalithic things, for some really fantastic reasons.

Millions of year's man wondered the forests of the world scavenging and foraging where ever we could. One of the important questions that anthropologists and anatomists have pondered for years is why did we develop the ability to walk upright. After all it is the least effective and efficient mode of transport. How did we survive millions of years before we miraculously developed tools to hunt with? Maybe we just suddenly developed these abilities because we were taught, or maybe we just arrived. OK: you got me. I don't really think that is what happened but I do think that there is life out there. I do believe that life did exist on Mars, and without a doubt I feel that we have and are being visited. Why? I do not know.

What discussion about UFOs would be complete without discussing at least in part Roswell, and Area 51? In July 1947 something crashed in Roswell New Mexico. That much of the story is: a fact. It's the rest of the story that leaves everyone asking questions. This is a classic example of how the truth is just the best policy. I have always believed that if the military and the government would have just told the public what it was right off the bat, no one would even remember the name of the town Roswell. Since the weather balloon theory has been so ridiculed and scoffed at; I began to wonder what it could be that the government wanted so badly to hide.

I personally find it very difficult to believe that our government held an experimental weather balloon secret for fifty years. The more and more I thought about it the more I realized that there is only one real plausible reason to hold the contents of this crash secret. There is something that the government fears more than UFOs and that is failure to secure our borders. I believe that the craft that crashed was not an American aircraft at all. It was in my opinion an aircraft from one of our enemies such as Russia, or China.

Think about it! In the 90's the Air Force released a statement about this Top Secret weather balloon designed to spy on Russian missile sites. Do you really think that the Russians weren't doing the same? For our government to openly admit that a foreign air craft invaded our airspace and either crashed or was shot down, would be synonymous with admitting that we are vulnerable. To admit this to the American public could have catastrophic consequences.

Area 51: It's such a colorful name that it invokes the air of secrecy and intrigue. It is no wonder to me that there are so many myths about Area 51. The name itself sounds like something out of a James Bond movie. I have already stated that I do believe in UFOs and alien visitors, but I do not buy the idea that we have portions or pieces of their technology. That theory in itself is preposterous. That would suggest that somehow we are smarter, faster, or just more fortunate then the other countries of the world. If we had alien technology we would be rubbing the world's nose in it. Telling everyone; "Look what we have."

So as much as I do believe in alien visitation, I also do not believe that every story is valid or true. Some experts claim that about 90 to 95 percent of all sightings can be explained. What I am referring to is that last 5 percent and I just don't believe that Roswell or Area 51 fall into those criteria. I also believe that many of the sightings are or at least could be experimental aircraft, but not all.

For example when a combat pilot sees something that is unidentifiable and unexplained, I tend to believe them. They are highly trained at identifying other aircraft and assessing the potential threat. I would hate to think that a combat pilot out there could somehow mistake a civilian airliner for a UFO. If that were to happen, how long before somebody gets shot down. It is just not likely that when the military encounters these unknown objects, they are probably the best observers to say whether it is real or not. In combat your life depends on your ability to assess the situation; there is no room for mistakes.

Last I would comment on Bob Lazar, who supposedly worked at Groom Lake. In my opinion, this guy is the biggest fraud that I have ever seen. For all of you true UFO believers you can increase your credibility by doing some home work and just stop buying the stories by people like him. Anyone truly interested in investigating this type of phenomenon I think it is prudent to be skeptical and cautious. There are idiots out there like Bob Lazar that have mundane useless lives that are looking for their moment of fame. For those of us that do believe, I think we need to not jump to conclusions and look at things from all angles, because that 5 percent are out there and we will eventually find proof.

One of my favorite mysteries is the infamous Bermuda Triangle. The first recorded incident in the Bermuda Triangle was written down in Christopher Columbus on the 11th of October 1492 on his way to the new world. Columbus reported that his compass was erratic and he reported seeing strange moving objects in the sky. From that time forward many mariners would report many things. At least those that came back to report anything. These were the tails of drunken sailors and nothing more for centuries.

By the mid-eighteen hundreds we started to keep better track of our ships and cargo. It was only a matter of time before a pattern seemed to emerge. A pattern that wasn't easy to ignore. It wouldn't be until the latter half of the twentieth century before we had a name for the place, but that had nothing to do with the disappearances. Before it had the name that we all recognize, it was called many things, such as: the Sea of Lost Souls, the Devils Triangle, and plenty of other colorful names.

The most important reason that we should investigate the Bermuda Triangle Phenomenon is the fact that without a doubt ships and planes do go missing. With ships and planes going missing, that undoubtedly means people go missing. So whether you think there is a mystery or not, there are lives being lost.

Lives like the ones in the famous flight of Flight 19 that left Ft. Lauderdale Florida on 5th of December 1945. Lt. Col. Charles C. Taylor led a flight of five Avenger Torpedo Bombers on a training mission and flew off into myth and legend. Many people know the story and there are about as many opinions about what really happened as there are people that know the story. There is however some interesting things that always gets my attention when I think about the subject.

First we have to look at the fact that Lt. Col. Taylor was an experienced combat pilot of WWII and an experienced trainer. Second would be that fact that the military is meticulous when it comes to the maintenance of its aircraft. Third we have the fact that it was good weather. Fourth is the fact that there were four other pilots, all with experience flying in this area. The last thing that I find interesting and probably most mysterious aspect of the story is the fact that these types of planes have a crew of three each. The official record shows that only fourteen people went missing that day.

With all this in mind, a person should have to ask themselves how an experienced combat pilot got lost is beyond my ability to comprehend. There is no mention in the recorded transcripts about mechanical malfunction other than the compass. Apparently the compass on all five aircraft had the same malfunction. If there was any question as to the ability of Lt. Col. Taylors mental state the next ranking pilot would have the authority and the responsibility to take command. Last is the idea that they went up missing a man. I find it very hard to believe that this would have happened. That is just not how the military does things. There are a couple of very important questions that need to be answered in conjunction with that fact. The first question is did the flight actually take off missing a crew member? If so why was the flight allowed to go on the mission with a missing man? Last is if they weren't missing a man who was he and where is the fifteenth crew member?

These are classic questions that I have when thinking about the Bermuda Triangle. The famous Mary Celeste is another one in which people fail to ask some important questions. If one is to believe the story that depicts that there was still hot coffee in the galley and uneaten food on the table and no sign of trouble what happened to them. Nobody knows what happened, but what concerns me is the coffee. If it was still warm then the crew and passengers could not be far away. So whether they panicked and jumped overboard or were taken prisoner by pirates there would have been signs and should have still been visible.

Planes and ships do not just disappear without a trace, or a call for help. What kind of catastrophic event must there be in order to bring a ship or plane to the bottom without a cry for help? Planes and ships also leave oil slicks and other debris when they go down where are these in the cases in the Bermuda Triangle. Why are these ships and planes so hard to find? With modern radar and all the technology that we have it should be easy to find at least a debris field or some sign of what happened. Recently when Air France Flight 447 crashed off the coast of Rio they were already finding and collecting debris and bodies within twenty four hours. But as recently as 1999 a research vessel called

Genesis disappeared in the Bermuda Triangle with all 3 crew and no trace was ever found.

Just as with UFOs, not all of the Bermuda Triangle disasters are mysteries, but some are: As is the case with the aforementioned Flight 19 and Mary Celeste. Some are simple and more understandable than others but it's the truly mysterious that need to be focused on. Several of these ships and planes were in fact in contact with control towers or other vessels right up to the time they disappeared. We must never just shrug our shoulders and say OH well, we did all we could. If we can't find them and we can't investigate what happened, we can't prevent it. That should be the point.

From here to the afterlife: I find it fascinating when I talk to people that believes in god but does not believe in ghosts. It would seem to me that one should go with the other. I know this isn't the case for everyone but the number is surprising. I would venture to say that the proof of ghosts would be the ultimate proof of life after death, and proof of a soul. Religious or not, there is a certain inherent need to try to understand what happens after we die. What a novel idea if we could prove that nothing happens, we just go on in ghost form.

There are not many people that I personally know that have not had an encounter of some kind. Footsteps on the stairs, a shadow out of place, or a whisper in the dark, are all simple things that many, many people have encountered. Yet; the overwhelming fear to admit that it may be the spirit of someone that has died is profound in itself.

Every culture, from every country, from all of recorded history has talked of and believed in ghosts. Some of those cultures simply accept them as fact, such as India. England's ghosts have been clearly documented and for the most part accepted for centuries. This tells me that as Americans we fear the idea of being the same as anything or anyone. It is as if in order to prove how different and truly enlightened we are we have to ignore everything that isn't easy to explain. Look at the reality of it: there is more evidence to support the evidence of ghosts than there is to prove the Big Bang. In the case of ghosts we have photos, eyewitness testimony, and paranormal investigators reports, the Big Bang has a mathematical equation, and nothing more.

When it comes to the unexplained and mysterious, it seems to scare people away from serious study, because of scientific ridicule. The scientist should be the first ones to encourage people to search for the truth in anything. In 1822 when Mary Ann Man discovered a strange tooth and showed to her husband Gideon, neither one had any idea that they had made one of the most important discoveries in world history. When proclaimed it to be the tooth of a giant lizard however he was mocked and accused of misinterpretation. Now they were not the first to find dinosaurs bones, in fact people were finding them for thousands of years. They were thought to belong to dragons and giants from some far gone time.

They were considered to be myth and legend, but one day someone would come along and decide to take serious look at them and that lead to the discovery of dinosaurs. Just like today none of the "serious" scientist would even investigate the subject while a common dentist took interest and eventually Richard Owen would discover that they were not lizards at all. They were much older and much bigger and paleontology was born. What about the first person to suggest the earth was round or the earth was not the center of the universe. These people were scrutinized and ridiculed and in some cases even put in prison for their ideas. I find it unbelievable that hundreds of years later nothing has changed.

Chapter II

Conspiracy Theories

Your average conspiracy theorist is as guilty at propagating false information as the people they claim are the criminals. We all need to remember; propaganda is the truth, from a certain point of view. The greatest propagator of deception comes from our own beliefs, desires, and expectations.

I am not one to fall for conspiracy theories very easily, but some are pretty compelling. Some are just silly, and some are completely preposterous. I will try to address some of each. I doubt that I will be able to solve any of them but maybe I can create some plausible theories for the implausible. I hope that my theories will make more sense than the "magic bullet theory," or that coincidence and bad luck can explain the unexplained. I do not believe in coincidence or luck, either good or bad. I believe that everything happens for a reason.

Conspiracy theories are like an infectious disease, the infection starts as a small cut or scrape and then it festers and grows until it is a serious problem. The ironic aspect of this metaphor is that just like that cut or scrape, if people take care of it early on it goes away. Picture if you will that you live in a place where you are not allowed bandaging wounds. Infection and disease would spread like wildfire. That is one of the downfalls of free speech. In other words, it doesn't need to be factual to be reported.

I love freedom of speech, and I believe in the right of anyone and everyone to have that right. There are times however, when the propaganda and theoretical ideology leave commonsense and reason behind. That is when I would rather just not hear about it.

When it comes to the seriously stupid conspiracies there is simply no fix. Freedom of speech insures that every idiot in the country can say whatever they want whether it is based in fact or not. In this, I exercise my freedom of speech and say, all that profit from lies, discontent, and the fabrication of conspiracies are the worst terrorists. I refer to these people as "Capitalist Terrorists" or Capitalism Terrorism." These people like to take a tragic event and then turn it around, twist it, and discredit everyone and everything, just to make a buck. Even the Jihadists believe in what they are doing. These idiots are only doing it because they love the sound of their own voice and/or for profit.

To be specific, I am referring to the worst pathetic attempt at a conspiracy I have ever heard, and that is the 9/11 conspiracy. It is my full hearted opinion that the perpetrators of this conspiracy are the most irrational, amateurish, wretched human beings that ever lived. For those that are educated: they are an insult to the rest of the educated world, and don't disserve the oxygen that they waste every day that they live; to say nothing of the space they take up.

I begin with the one that offends me the most: Dylan Avery, the writer and director of the documentary "Loose Change". After watching his video I wasn't sure if he was insane or just stupid. So I had to check out what the web had to say. On his web-site in his bio section it turns out that he is a failed film student. Who was turned down twice from film school, and I can see why. I have seen dogs and cats with more talent than he has. He did on the other hand have something going for him. He was willing and capable of turning an American tragedy into a joke complemented by the beliefs of the feeble minded, and topped it all off with making money. In a capitalist society everything is acceptable so long as you can sell it.

I refer to people such as Dylan Avery as terrorists because of the simple dictionary definition of terrorism: "The use of terror against a person or group." If the act of trying to convince the people of this country that our government not only could but would fabricate 9/11 for some dire conspiracy is terrifying. Therefore they are terrorists in my opinion.

Now I will admit that our government has several black ops and black projects that we will never know about, but I personally believe that the wholesale murder of American citizens and destruction of

U.S. property are very unlikely and unbelievable. There are simply some things that are beyond what they are capable of or willing to do: assuming they could get the organizations that would be needed to go alone in the first place. I mean here's the scenario: [picture the president telling the people involved] "I have an idea; I want to fake an attack on the World Trade Center, The Pentagon, and The White House. I want it to look like terrorists, and most important I want it to raise oil prices so I can fund my retirement." Does anybody really believe this crap?

Let's look at this from a different point of view. Let's assume for a minute that Dylan Avery is right. What does that tell us? It tells me a couple of things. First I would have to say that if he is correct in his assumptions he should be afraid, very afraid. A government that is not only willing but capable of pulling off a grand conspiracy of this nature sure wouldn't be afraid of making a couple of punk ass wannabe cinematographers disappear. If the people involved in propagating these types of conspiracy theories were to suddenly all die mysteriously; it would lend a certain amount of credibility to their theory.

Then there is the fact that they saw through the government veil and they alone were capable of discovering what no one else was capable of seeing. Maybe they can see through the secrecy because they were in on it? Maybe they are the terrorists that helped plan it? If someone comes forward with inside information during a criminal investigation, they would probably be added to the suspect list.

Anyone with any common sense can see straight through their bullshit. This is just a case of a group of kids who are capitalizing on other people's grief to make a buck, nothing more. There simply is not one thing in their video that can be validated by any professional from any field. Their so called experts are probably college drop outs or failures themselves.

I have never been so personally offended in my life; in fact I am not totally sure that I have ever been offended in that way. I personally think that the people involved with the making of "Loose Change" should be held and tried for treason. These are the same Neo-Nazi Communist Islamic Extremists that think things such as the Holocaust didn't happen, because it was just propaganda. I rank these guys and their followers' right up there with the people that ran the prison camps of Auschwitz and Dachau. In the goal of making money they create discord, discontent and mistrust, and they do it all with lies. If I were them and truly believed what they are selling, I would be looking over my shoulder, after all, if our government can pull that off???

There are some theories that are less absurd, but none the less just as false. We have stories such as the Moon Landing Conspiracy, and the WWII conspiracy. The Moon Landing Conspiracy believers think that the famed Moon landing never happened and that it was filmed in a Hollywood film set. For the WWII Conspiracy the belief is that we knew the Japanese were going to attack and let it happen so we could enter the war.

I will tackle the moon landing first. To me it sounds completely ludicrous, but it is still more plausible than the 9/11 theory. More possible because of the fact that it didn't harm anyone, wasn't perpetrated for detrimental outcomes, it could be done with minimal security risk, and it was a victorious event that people could rally around. The United States were number one. Low cost, no harm, and a lot of positive press, so even if it was fallacious, I say who cares? I don't see how whether it was valid or not changes anything.

The proponents have several good arguments and a few relatively interesting facts, but we again have to look at the whole of the theory not just the parts that support the hoax. To get to the bottom of any conspiracy we need to start at the beginning. In this case we have Bill Kaysing who was an employee for Rocketdyne. (The company that made the engine for the Saturn V Rocket) Bill was not an engineer or a scientist; he did have a BA Degree in English and worked for Rocketdyne as a writer and librarian. He wrote a book entitled: "We Never Went to the Moon, Americas 30 Billion Dollar Swindle".

Before we dive into the theories let me point out a common thread to the 9/11 theory. The 9/11 theory was produced by a wannabe filmmaker, and the Moon Landing Hoax was perpetrated by a wannabe writer. Both made money off their hypothetical data by discrediting and clouding serious and significant events of their time. As we look at several of these theories, I will make this connection on many of them. Such is the case with Bart Sibrel the film maker that made the film entitled "A Funny Thing Happened on the Way to the Moon": Just another person that jumped on the band wagon to make a buck. Critics may point out that I am doing the same thing by writing about it myself. Yes: I am doing exactly that, with the distinction that I am not trying to mislead anyone in doing it.

I also find it interesting as to who believes in such rubbish. According to some polls of 18 – 25 year olds approximately 25 percent think it was erroneous. Why could that be? These people live in the digital age of video games, high definition television, and movies with graphics that are more real than real life; it doesn't surprise me at all to think they might believe it could be falsified. Then there are the 28 percent of Russians that don't believe it happened. Of course they don't believe it they were the loser of the space race. They are not the only people to have ever claimed that the other team cheated and that made them the loser.

I will admit that the technology existed and the political ambition existed to perpetrate just such a hoax, however just because it is possible doesn't make it accurate. As I acknowledged earlier there are some interesting points that the proponents assert. Bart Sibrel claims the reason for the hoax was to distract from the Vietnam War. His evidence is the fact that we landed on the Moon at the height of the war and the stopped the program about the same time as we pulled out of Vietnam.

There are a couple of flaws in his proposal. First: 1968 was the worst year in the Vietnam War; some of the highest death rates of the war were in the early months of 1968 not the middle of 1969. Second: We pulled out of Vietnam for the same reason that we suspended the space program: Money. Just like today, too many people are worried about what the war costs and not enough about bringing it to a victorious close. Equally so there has been much discussion about the future of the space program, I for one believe that it is one thing that we could cut from our budget, at least for now.

Many of the claims are politically motivated and in that I can understand, I don't necessarily trust the motives of our politicians either. I don't completely trust anyone with that much power. Does that mean that our government perpetrated a conspiracy for dark personal achievement? I don't know! It has been claimed that this hoax was perpetrated for Cold War prestige, financial gain, and even misdirection of funding to divert money through NASA to the military. Again there are some common themes in the motives that are not so different than the 9/11 theory.

There are some thoughts that I find compelling and fascinating. I am not a physicist so the answers to these questions are probably beyond my ability to theorize, but I do feel that there is some simple answers non-the-less. I must admit that the question of the golf ball slicing is intriguing. When the astronauts teed off on the moon the joke was made that he sliced the ball. For this to happen there needs to be an atmosphere. Since the spin on the ball reacts with the air and causes it to curve it makes the ball slice one way or the other. There is no air on the moon, so how is this possible?

I remember a simple experiment when I was a child in which you have two children sitting on a marry-go-round and one kid throws a ball to the other. No matter how hard you try, you can't seem to throw the ball straight to the other person, because visually it appears to turn in mid flight. If you look at the throw from above in slow motion photography you clearly see that the ball went straight, it was just your perception that is off. I think that it is possible that this is the case with the golf ball. The Moon is rotating as well as traveling around the Earth and therefore the astronaut's perception of the flight path of the ball made it appear to curve.

Then there are the camera angles. When we see Neil Armstrong coming down the ladder on the Lander, the question is who was filming this event? Great question but it is my theory that no one was, it was probably filmed from a remote camera on the Rover that landed first or from a remote controlled camera on the Lander itself. There are several camera angle issues but all of them can be explained trough the fact that they had remote controlled cameras built into their suits. Just because you don't see them running around with a Polaroid doesn't make it fictitious.

Where are all the stars in the photos? This is just a case of; not being able to see the forest because of all the trees. Because there is no atmosphere and the sun is so bright it simply blots out the stars and therefore makes them virtually invisible to the naked eye. Many times there are just simple explanations to even the most bizarre questions. That seems to be part of the problem in many cases. The fact that so many things have simple and un-complicated answers makes people feel as if there is something wrong with the conclusions. We as people have a tendency to make things complicated and when they are not, we need to make them more complex than they really are.

I feel that this is true in the case of the WWII conspiracy. The Conspiracy holds that President Roosevelt knew about the attack on Pearl Harbor and decided to do nothing just so we would have an excuse to enter the war. It is true that the war was widely unpopular and the

American public opposed the U.S. entering into the conflict. It was generally believed that it was a European problem and that it was not our predicament. [Sound familiar] We were just starting to drag our way out of the Great Depression and the cost of entering into a war that was not our trouble was just not very accepted.

Just as in the case of the Moon Landing I say that this conspiracy is plausible, but doubtful. Again this type of theory is based on the idea that we are so great and all knowing, we must ask how it is possible that we could be attacked without our government knowing. Simple answers bring complicated theories and dark motives. There is a propensity just as in the 9/11 theory that we are simply too powerful to let something like this happen unless there are other powers at work. Paradoxically it is that type of thinking that allows for enemies of the U.S. to make us victims. Many times it appears to me that every time we think we are too powerful to be challenged, we get proven wrong.

Here are some of the facts that are involved in both the theory and the rebuttal. Prior to the attack on the base at Pearl Harbor, the United States Navy moved their carrier fleet out on maneuvers. Doing this left primarily World War I battleships and cruisers left in the harbor. The base was in a stand down status and leave was given to anyone that wished to take advantage of it, and wanted it.

A couple of days prior to this' there had been a report of a large fleet on the move in the North West Pacific. According to some this report reached as high as the White House. In the early hours of 7 December 1941 messages were intercepted that suggested that an attack was imminent. At 7:55 Hawaii time the sirens rang. The blame for the attack fell entirely on Adm. H.E. Kimmel and Gen. W. Short for failing to respond. Proponents of the theory state that the reason that they bore the brunt of the criticism was because the rest of the brass was in Washington D.C. attending an important meeting.

The true blame here is the technology, timing, and human error. The information was available to detect and respond to the attack. The timing failed, even the Japanese ambassador didn't know until after the attack, that Japan had declared war on the United States. Human error plays its part in all true tragedies. There were plenty of signs that could have prevented 9/11, there were plenty more that could have prevented the Ft. Hood Massacre, but those signs only matter if someone is willing and capable of seeing, reading, and acting on what they see. As we know from countless examples we don't like it when people interpret what they think is going to happen, it is just better to wait and see.

FDR did not know per say that we were going to be attacked. He probably was advised that somebody thought that we were going to be attacked. Whether he did or he didn't, makes no difference to me. Assuming that he took this advice serious and sent a task force to intercept the Japanese, then what? We attack and kill hundreds of Japanese sailors and we are accused of a pre-emptive strike and they declare war. We talk to their ambassadors and ask what they are doing, and request that they back off the fleet; and we do it really nicely. By the time the message is received the attack would already be over. We could have put the base on alert, and instead of 2,000 casualties there may have been ten times as many, because everyone would have been at their duty stations.

I think that FDR was oblivious to the threat just as most of our leaders are today. Even if he was aware I don't think that it would have changed anything, because that is the way people like it. We are a nation that reacts and are afraid of being proactive at anything. There is no conspiracy involving Pearl Harbor just complacency. We could have prevented the attack by simply staying out of Japanese business in Manchuria, and maybe not torpedoing their ships in the North China Sea. We could have avoided the whole thing if we just turned the other cheek and pretended that it wasn't happening.

Complacency and ignorance are the destroyers of nations. War was coming either way. That was decided the minute our country had an opinion on what was going on in the world. To avoid this in the future we need to look at all possible outcomes and repercussions, but most importantly, we need to realize that those threats are real. I wonder, however, how the Jews and the rest of Europe would view us today had we listened to the nearly 80% of Americans that thought we should avoid the war.

I briefly mentioned it earlier but the fact is that 80%: yes 80% of Americans opposed the war. That is more than opposed Vietnam, Korea, or any war since. Yet we feel all justified because we helped prevent genocide, and world domination by a dictator. [After the fact] We love nothing more than to claim victory when we didn't want to help in the first place. After all we were only helping because of some conspiracy to raise gas prices, become a world power, and/or take our place in the world stage. It couldn't possibly be because we were attacked and people like Hitler needed to be stopped; it couldn't possibly be for those reasons could it? I wish the people that believe conspiracies like this would stop being so blind. To anyone that believes in these types of conspiracies: I ask, the next time you talk to a Jewish Concentration Camp survivor; you explain to them that the only reason we helped was because we were tricked.

There is one Conspiracy that has always intrigued me and probably always will. That is the Kennedy assassinations. The Kennedy family had a long and sorted past full of money, greed, and politics. [Not a good combination] To be clear and honest, I have no love for the Kennedy family or their politics, but I do feel that out of all the conspiracies that I have read, this is the only one that may be true. I emphasize maybe true. There are certainly some aspects that are hard to quantify. Before we look at JFK however let's look at what all lead up to these events.

With any conspiracy there is always more than meets the eye, and in my opinion the roots of the conspiracy run deep and many directions. For the Kennedy's these roots started with Joseph P. Kennedy Sr. who was a colorful determined man himself, and just like his sons later, made his own enemies. Joe Kennedy was born on the 6th of September 1888, was educated at Harvard. Joe went into business at a young age and in his early years made his name and his money by running Rum during Prohibition and investing in the stock market. His insider trading activities which were not illegal at that time made him a formidable trader and investor. According to some he was also involved in the "Bear Raid" which led to the stock market crash of 1929. (Bear Raid: Is a strategy by which a person or group or persons artificially cause the market to fall for the purpose of buying low: A form of securities fraud today.)

Joe then started to get involved in politics when he became the Chairman of the Securities and Exchange Commission from 1934 to 1935. He then was appointed U. S. Ambassador to the United Kingdom in 1938 and held that post until 1940. It was during his post as Ambassador that, in my opinion, his true colors and ambitions started to show. During his post he learned to enjoy the high status of a high profile position.

When World War II started in 1939 and then came to England, he openly supported Hitler. While addressing the press Joseph P. Kennedy Sr. stated: "Democracy is finished in England. It may be here."

[Referring to the U.S.] He also once stated that there is nothing wrong with being on the winning side, again referring to Hitler. Joe was seen by many in both England and the United States as a defeatist and could not be trusted to act in the name of the U.S. He strongly opposed the war and he in fact thought that we should not only stay out of it, but we should have opened dialog with Hitler. Later, Joe's friend would write and talk about his anti-semantic views, pointing out that he was very anti-Jew in his opinions.

With all of these points of view made public and part of the record, his dreams of being President were finished and more so when the U.S. won the war that he thought was not winnable by the Allies. For the first time in his career he gambled on the wrong side, and it cost him big. This didn't mean however that he didn't plan for that eventuality.

He had already got his sons into the military. He was in my opinion playing both sides. If Germany won he could say "I told you so" and if America won, he had the boys in place to be heroes. He knew if one of the Kennedy's were going to be President they would have to be "on the winning side."

During the war Joe Jr. was assigned to the Army Air Corp and during Operation Aphrodite he was killed when his B-24 went missing over Europe. The bomber had been heavily loaded with explosives and the flying bomb that he was piloting prematurely exploded. The family banner and Joe Sr.'s hopes now fell to John. John joined the Navy and became the Captain of a PT boat in the Pacific. While Captaining PT 109, John and his crew were struck broadside by a Japanese Destroyer killing two of his crew. He managed to rescue the rest. Joe Sr. saw this as the opportunity he was waiting for and made sure that he was decorated for his efforts. Later when JFK was asked how he became a hero he replied: "They sank my boat."

John F. Kennedy Jr. was assassinated on 22nd of November 1963 when he was shot in the head by an assassin's bullet. However that year was an interesting year for the Kennedy's. All of which could play into the conspiracy that this chapter is about. There are a couple of things that for me just leave questions in my mind every time I think about the Kennedy assignation. I have studied the evidence and listened to the testimony of witnesses.

Here are the facts that bother me. The bullet that killed Kennedy was found on the stretcher next to his body. The first bullet that hit him had enough kinetic energy and muzzle velocity to travel through his upper torso, the seat in front of him, through Sen. Conley's wrist, and finally into his leg. The second bullet, according to the Warren Commission entered the back of his head but did not exit. It is my experience that muscle slows a bullet more than a skull. If the bullet didn't travel through the skull, why was it found on the stretcher?

Second major problem I have is the footage from the Zapruder film. I have watched it and watched it and it doesn't matter how many ways it gets explained, it just doesn't hold to any level of reality. Now I have seen the computer recreations, the guy that shoots the pig and all sorts of ballistic jell that never proved anything. Using the same ammunition shot by this rifle. In all of that they can recreate the shot, the trajectory, and the impact, but they can't recreate the reality. At that range the bullet has more than enough muzzle velocity to enter and exit the human skull. A frozen pig skull or even a natural pig skull isn't a fare comparison, because the skull is thicker, harder and if it is dead and frozen it is full of a much more condensed substance than brain matter.

In the experiment in which the expert shot the dead pig I was instantly unimpressed, because I have shot pigs before with similar rifles of the period at even greater range and the bullet had no problem entering and exiting the head of the pig. In fact there is something else that I have noticed several times when I shot and killed something and that is the bodily reaction to the impact, as well as the entry and exit wounds.

When you shoot a living thing in the head, the head almost always moves away from the direction in which the shot came from. The entry wound is small and clean in the case of a military full metal jacketed bullet. The exit wound on the other hand is generally very violent. When the bullet exits, it has expanded and tumbled and will explode from the other side, leaving a huge crater. When I watch the footage of the kill shot, what I see is Kennedy's head violently move back, and you can clearly see a chunk of matter fly up and to the rear.

This is further complicated by the fact that the autopsy report claims that there was only a dime size hole on the back of Jack's head. If the bullet entered the back of the head the hole should have been 6.5 mm or in other words, about quarter that size. If the bullet entered from the back, why did his head move back? What was this piece of debris that flew off the back of his head? Last, how come the bullet was found outside of a head that it never exited?

It has also always bothered me that so much of the original evidence has "disappeared" since the assassination. Lee Harvey Oswald, the biggest failure of the twentieth century, who probably couldn't plan and execute a trip to the grocery store. He was a piss poor soldier, and a communist, but if he was even involved in the assassination he was a patsy. Then you got Jack Ruby, a wannabe gangster who thought he could make a name for himself but quickly died in prison. [How convenient] The whole thing played out like a bad Hollywood movie.

There are so many reasons for this to be a conspiracy that it is hard to count them all. Why would anyone want to kill the great Kennedy's? I say what was so great about them? In 1963 alone they were responsible for enough chaos and death to start several wars; it doesn't surprise me that somebody got through the security. Let's look at some of the things that Jack and Bobby were involved in that may have caused someone to want them assassinated.

Starting in early 1961, Kennedy began to increase the number of advisors in Vietnam, and in 1962 committed the first combat troops to help stop the spread of communism. On the 1st of November of 1963, he sanctioned a coup to over throw President Diem of Vietnam, which resulted in Diem's death. That same year, the Kennedy's sanctioned and supported a coup in Iraq in support of the Ba'ath Party, a revolt that Suddam Hussein participated and eventually gained power because of. The Kennedy's sanctioned and authorized the assassination of Fidel Castro, and during the Cuba Missile Crisis, Jake Kennedy brought us closer to nuclear war than any leader of any country in the world.

After Jacks death, Bobby went on to shake the tree of discord around the United States and the world. With his crusade against organized crime and the teamsters, he might just as well of painted a bull's eye on his forehead. In 1967 he supported the Israeli 6 Day War against the Palestinians, and even though he supported the civil rights movement he authorized wire taps of Dr. Martin Luther King Jr. to determine if he had communist connections. In the interest of national security, he authorized the same sort of actions that President Bush did after 9/11, that we now consider being an attack on our civil liberties. When I made the statement that the Kennedy's had a sorted past I meant it, and the shining armor of Camelot is stained with the blood of many. Something that Dr. Martin Luther King Jr. said, I feel applies nicely to my feelings on the Kennedy's. I quote: *"Never forget that what Hitler did in Germany was legal."*

Navigating Insanity

There was no shining light of Camelot nor should there be. The Kennedy's were every bit as corrupt and power hungry as any politician, to say nothing of their greedy self indulgence, and sexual urges, that even Tiger Woods can't get away with today. Conspiracy or no conspiracy, there is one thing that money can't buy or protect you from, and that is the vengeance of someone that feels they have been wronged. They thought that they were above the law and beyond the reach of mortal men, and in both cases were brought down none the less. In their case I do believe that greed kills.

In all conspiracies one only needs to ask: who will benefit most from the conspiracy. In many cases the only people that benefit are the people perpetrating the conspiracy. In my first two examples we see people that are basically failures in life who need to capitalize on other people's misery and suffering. In my last example of JFK, there are people out there that can and will revenge and I feel that Kennedy's pushed a lot of buttons all at the wrong time. There arrogance killed them that much, I am sure.

In the case of the Kennedy's, there are many that were probably happy and indeed did profit from their demise, but in the first two the theorists are the only ones that have anything to gain from their arguments. If we proved tomorrow that Pearl Harbor or the Moon landings were somehow part of a conspiracy what would it matter. As for 9/11 if they somehow proved it to be true, they would probably be responsible for starting another civil war that would result in more death then the war they proclaim to be opposed to.

"Fear not the path of truth for the lack of people walking on it."
Robert Kennedy 5 June 1968

"In the end, we will not remember the words of
our enemies, but the silence of our friends."
Dr. Martin Luther King Jr.

"A man that won't die for something is not fit to live."
Dr. Martin Luther King Jr.

Chapter 12

Leadership/Management

Never fire someone on a holiday or birthday.
Take the time to know who it is you are relieving and letting go.
A yes man is only that; nothing more.

Overtime produces three types of people.
There are ones that needs the money who can't manage their own finances.
There are ones that wants the money, because they are greedy.
Finally; there are ones that don't want to be there.
(None of which are profitable or necessary to the company.)

To maximize profit: Hold you managers to the highest
of standards, and eliminate overtime.

The skill of leadership is a gift that is not given to most, but there is always the possibility that it can be earned. Leadership is not bestowed by a title; it is demonstrated and ultimately earned through ones actions. Someone may be the highest ranked individual at a firm, or location, or even a country. None of this makes them a leader. I abhor it when people refer to our elected officials as leaders. I have yet to see even one that is qualified to bare that title. This is true of most corporate executives as well. What most, if not all of the aforementioned people are; are managers, nothing more. Some may say that they are both the same. My 1stSgt when I was in the Army said it best. Managers are like sheepherders; any jack ass can manage, but only a leader can inspire people to rise above and be the best they can be.

Management is the art of categorizing and labeling. Deciding who works where, doing what. Many people are great managers. They balance their check books, manage their finances, manage their time, and their families but they are not leading anything. This makes them little more than logistic clerks.

Managing is the act of telling someone what to do and when to do it. Leadership is deciding what needs to be done and then demonstrating how to do it. Managers command from their office and work specific hours. Leaders command in person and are the first to show up and the last to leave.

Leaders are the people that always consider what would be best, even if it isn't popular. Sometimes leaders are forced to make bad decisions, such as sending men and women into harm's way. One cannot manage people in combat, but if you have the courage, one can lead them into battle. This is the simplest way to determine the different between a leader and a manager.

Throughout history leaders have led their people and this country through some of the most horrible of circumstances. Presidents such as Roosevelt, Wilson, and Lincoln will be remembered for centuries. How many people do you know that can tell you the name of the CEO's for General Motors or AIG? Chances are not many. The reason for this is because instead of leading their people and companies through hardship they managed them. They managed by begging for funds from the American people. That is management.

In business there is a lot of emphasis on management, and there are many classes that one can take for the same subject. Management is useful, but should never be considered a role of entitlement. Rather it is a role of leadership that has gotten misguided over the years. Managers love to refer to their crews, employees, and workers as a team. The popular phrase is there is no "I" in team, unless they are talking about themselves.

If your boss asks you to work overtime, but refuses to do so themselves; rooted entirely in some ideology of entitlement, then there is no team, because they just put "I" into the equation. In this situation a manager would tell you that they are paid salary and that it is not their job to do overtime. It is all right for you because you get paid time and a half. A leader would be there by your side, because they realize that if they are necessary eight hours a day, then they are necessary during overtime as well.

Companies can't just preach teamwork, they need to perform and function as a team. The reason that management is paid salary is that it entitles them to overtime pay even if they don't work overtime, but when it is needed then they need to work it. Too many of these types of managers have come to think that they deserve it.

This is much of the problem with executive bonuses and all of the problems on Wall Street. These executives have come to think they are entitled to these bonuses and extraordinary pay, but they are both tied to performance. When a company is performing well, I believe that the people responsible for the increase in revenue be rewarded, but when the opposite is true then they need to be held accountable. They would argue that there are upswings and downturns in the market and that it is unfair to hold executives responsible for things they can't control. I say that is the reason they are executives. They exist to deal with these types of events. It's as if they think they should get credit for success, but be absolved from blame for failure, because it is beyond their control.

We know the economy goes up and down in almost regular cycles. A good manager or leader should always be planning for the next down turn, instead of assuming that the high that they may be riding will last forever. This is the case of Lehman Bro. when they recorded record earnings and paid 10 million in dividends just nine months before they filed Chapter 11 bankruptcy. Good leadership could have prevented this while poor management clearly and undoubtedly caused it.

In history there were several great leaders, people of vision, dedication, and strength of will that have brought entire nations into greatness and others to their knees. People like Gaius Julius Caesar born 13th of July 100 BCE became ruler of the Empire of Rome in 44 BCE and reined until his assassination on the 15th of March 49 BCE, remembered 2000 years later as the Ides of March. His leadership is remembered to this day when on his birthday and the anniversary of his death people still leave flowers at his grave. 2000 years later people still honor him for what he created and what he did. His battle tactics are still studied and utilized today. That is leadership.

Alexander the Great is another of these leaders that deserve to be remembered. Alexander III of Macedon was born in 356 BCE, was king by the age of 18, ruler of the known world, and dead by the age of 32. Show me one Wall Street wannabe moron that can pull that off.

There are many more people such as Patton, Boyington, MacArthur,

Grant, Pershing, Washington, Diocletian, Attila, Genghis Khan, Boudicca, and so many more that we can't even begin to name them all. Leaders all: not managers; not one. This is part of the point of this chapter. I feel that we need to move from the concept of management to the concept of leadership. With true leadership we can achieve great things, move forward, and most importantly provide the people with something that we all need, hope: The hope that there is a positive future, the hope that we all can have the American Dream, and the hope that we can make a difference in the world.

Leadership verses management is actually a simple idea. Get rid of the unaccountability and make leaders stand up and be counted. As you read this it will probably have dawned on you that all the great leaders that I mentioned were military leaders. That is because in the military we work for the people under us as much as we work for the people above us. There is just too much greed and divergence of blame in the corporate world. This too is another difference between management and leadership. Management likes to divert and delegate the blame for any given situation. The military holds the person that failed to do something about the problem responsible, and equally rewards those who excel.

There are some simple solutions to this problem in the civilian world, but they won't like it. In the military we track a problem up to the person that had the ability to fix it and that person is disciplined. In the civilian world they work from the top down. They try to figure out who had control and responsibility, but the problem is that in many corporations there is no one person that makes decisions or have control of anything. The problem is the fact that too many departments want to take credit for the good stuff, but this also allows them to divert the blame when it all goes wrong.

To run a business or a corporation with the hopes of success we need to look at things differently. As an upper level manager we need to hold our other management to different standards. As a corporate executive we need to do the same. Most importantly the shareholders need to hold the company to a higher standard by making them earn their money rather than expect it. I have heard it said that a good CEO is like having the ultimate quarterback. If that were true then the company would treat the employees as team players and understand that without them the quarterback doesn't even matter.

Marketing without the production capability to build or what the sales can produce, has a negative outcome every time. Again this is not what I think of as team work. The typical quarterback is the "Hero" of any game, but he could not do anything if it wasn't for the rest of the "team." Your team could have the best quarterback in the division, but without the defense, receivers, and kickers they wouldn't stand a chance of winning a game. So why does the corporate world think that the quarterback is the only part of the team that matters.

Where would any team be without their fans, or in the corporate world; the customers? Here is a team concept for you. Most economists would agree that if you are to manage your home, you need to have at least six to nine months of savings. Corporations must do the same. I suggest that companies work the same as the rest of us. In the recent decline in GDP and the DOW all out of whack, many of these same people would argue that we the common citizen, should save and prepare for nine months of down turns. I say what if corporations needed to save nine months of expenditures, just in case of economic "Down Turns"?

It's not as simple as just acting like things are different, we must actually change things. As I mentioned in the previous paragraphs, we need to change our style as well as our thinking. Another place that we need to rethink is in our interpretations of importance. I have already discussed who is the most important in the company, but what these companies need to realize is that none of them are important. Not the CEO, CFO, COO, the shareholder's, stockholders, and certainly not the board of directors. No: The most important person in the company doesn't even work for the company. That person is the customer.

On the surface companies like to pretend that they know that, and even try real hard to inform us that they care about us, the products and services that they provide, and the affordability of their products. BULLSHIT! Corporations care about one thing and one thing only: MONEY. Now I am certainly not against money, but if it affects our ability to function as a human being, then I say to hell with it all. Corporations aren't the ones guilty in this case. People in general are consumed by the need to have things. The only way to get these things is with money. This leads people to do some of the dumbest things.

Businesses and people in general will sue for the most outrageous reasons. Lawsuits are not for the purpose of justice or punishment; they are for greed, nothing more. It's sort of like when a company claims that "Quality is job #1" or when they advertise that they are "an equal opportunity employer." Is it really possible to advertise something that is law, much less advertise it as a bonus? I thought that quality was "job one" in every company??? If you read their advertisements; they would have you believe that they are the only ones that have things like equal employment opportunities, and quality. If I was the CEO of any of these companies and my human resources or marketing presented this type of crap to me I would probably fire them on the spot.

What does a prospective employee really care about? They care about all of those things that are considered taboo to ask during an interview. A perspective employee wants to know: What are my hours? What will I be paid? How much time off do I get? What are my benefits? Why should I work for you? These are the questions that I want to know, and the same questions that I think all employees should be asking. If the average employee expects or wants to be treated like somebody that deserves their pay, we need to hold the companies to a higher standard.

They will tell you that we can hire anyone to fill this job. If that were true then why do they have an interview process? Why do they advertize and offer the benefits that they do? They do this to attract the best workers they can, while trying to be oblivious and in unimpressed at the same time. They wish to make you feel like they don't need you while trying to get the best person for the position, and do this at the least cost possible.

In their ads they will tell you anything that sounds positive and nothing that won't. Companies that don't pay worth a hoot will not advertize their starting wage. They will state that they pay a competitive wage or "we pay for experience." These are just polite ways of saying we don't want to pay crap. Then there are the benefits! They will advertise a full benefit package, rather than telling you what it really is, because it isn't worth the paper that it's written on. The companies that have a real benefit package will break it down and publicize what and who they cover and for how much. There is much to be learned from the "Help Wanted Ad" that a company details.

Now I will admit that advertising at a bar is not the best place to find acceptable candidates for your company, but it is a great place to find out how people feel about working for your company. At one of my former employers we were told that we couldn't wear our uniform shirts to the bar, because we were representatives of the company. However, it is a small town and everyone knows where everyone works, and frankly it was the best place to find out the true feelings of the employees.

While working for this same company they had a recruiting problem. The suggestion was made that if we just listened to why people didn't want to apply that maybe we could get more applicants. They said that bar talk was not a viable explanation for any of their problems. They failed to realize however that those drunk, ex-employees are the voice of the company; especially in a small town. If the workers are happy they will repeat it, if they are unhappy they will tell the world. You will always have the disgruntled employees that got fired, or "let go" for one reason or another, but it is the ones that quit that will kill your reputation as an employer.

This reputation starts to resemble the things that companies and corporations will not advertise, and in many cases even admit. Take some average company policies for example. Why not advertise that, "We are a no smoking facility." When a company that I worked for implemented a no smoking policy [for the purpose of promoting employee health] I asked why not advertise it. Promoting employee health is a positive thing, is it not? They implemented a drug testing policy, but didn't want to put in the ads, because they were worried about "scarring people away from applying." They are willing to advertise the fact that they pay overtime [which is the law] but they won't advertise how many hours you will be required to work.

Corporate advertising and marketing is designed: whether related to recruiting employees or customers, is all a lie and is based on your best hopes, not facts. Just like the aforementioned smoking policy or drug testing, companies shy away from those types of things because even though they don't want you to do them, they still need you to apply. For the truth, ask yourself: When was the last time you saw an ad that read like the following?

Help Wanted

An excellent job opportunity is waiting for you with XYZ Corp. Inc. A great work environment that includes:

- Full Time Employment
- We pay overtime (We do a lot, including Saturdays)
- No smoking
- No Talking

- 30 Minute lunch (including travel time to and from the break room)
- Absenteeism is unacceptable (even with a doctors excuse)
- A 1% per year raise, based on performance (Even when the cost of living raises 5%)
- Excellent health Insurance (if you can get them to pay, and you can afford the premiums and deductibles)
- 401K available if you have any money left (we match if we make enough)
- Mandatory overtime
- Mandatory drug testing for accidents
- We do background checks: Criminal Background, Credit Check, Facebook
- People that have made mistakes in life, have unpaid credit cards or medical bills, and might voice an opinion need not apply.

All this can be yours if you can pass a drug
test and back ground check.
If interested call; 1-800-EAT-MEEE (1-800-328-6333)

This is based on several real companies, the name and the phone number are obviously fabricated, I have many friends that work and have worked at places such as this and I can assure you that this is all true. Unfortunately, these types of circumstances are all too common. It is my bet that this company wouldn't get many applications if they told the truth. I personally know people that will not even apply, who have been out of work for more than a year, because of their reputation, and the facts speak loader than the rhetoric.

My point is that companies need to start to live up to their rhetoric and stop trying to fool everyone. They don't offer overtime as a benefit, it's a law. They don't care about what happened at home or why you're gone because they don't have to. This was made apparent to me when my wife got sick and they told me that they were required to make me use personal time and vacation before the FMLA would take effect, and when they told me that I needed a doctor's excuse for each absence. Since then I went to school for Business Management, Human Resources, and Business Law, as well as Accounting, and Education. I learned that everything they said was a lie. The company is allowed to make me use vacation and personal time, but it is not required, and most importantly it is not required to receive a doctors' excuse for each absence. Once an illness has been documented, one only needs to update it once a year.

Then there are the raises, and they are appalling and completely ridiculous. At a quarter a year the average employee with a company receives approximately 2-3% per year raise. Many years the cost of living increases around 5% and some costs such as medical expenditures can rise at much higher rates. To call a 3% raise a performance raise is an insult. Then if you don't like it they will tell you, "There is the door." That is like telling someone that they can jump off the cliff or get shot. Some choice! Workers could cripple this country if they stood together and just stopped showing up for work.

Let us look at some company policies and how they work. The corporation decides that they want to impose a no smoking policy because of health concerns, lost productivity, or some other crap. I have heard claims by employer's that had claims of countless hours of lost time due to people smoking. What they failed to calculate was the time they lost due to people waiting to the last minute to go back to work, sneaking out to have a smoke, and the time wasted taking people to the office to discipline them for disobeying the aforementioned policy. It's absolutely incredible to me to think that they would fire someone that had fifteen years experience because they caught them smoking. At the same time it is not surprising that I don't know of any that have, at least to my knowledge.

If they aren't going to enforce the policy, then why do they have it? Simple: They get a tax cut and insurance break for doing so. One of my favorite bits of business law is the fact that for a company policy to be enforceable, it must be adhered to 100% of the time. If so much as one person is or has gotten away with breaking the policy in which they think they are upholding they have no policy or legal ground to stand on. In other words, if employee X is getting away with smoking outside and has not been fired, then it is OK for employee Y to do the same. Rank within the company has no barring, and does not afford some privileges over others. A company policy applies to everyone. If the CEO can walk around the factory floor without safety glasses, so can everyone.

One of the most important and most disputed policies is attendances. The problem starts with the fact that the people that make the policies sit in an office. Sitting in an office is easy to do with a cold, headache, or sore back. They don't have to deal with lifting things, walking up and down ladders, or even loud noises and certainly not bad weather conditions. I have been on both sides of that desk, and I can tell you that most of these managers simply don't believe you when something is wrong. There is always an excuse. In fact I think they have more excuses then the employees. There are those that will take advantage of every situation, but that doesn't mean that all do. Strangely enough they think that every time someone calls in they must just be lazy or hung-over. When they make a decision, we think it is meant to screw us over somehow: Seems fair somehow.

Oddly enough companies don't and are not trying to screw anyone specifically except the customers. They do on the other hand try to fight change. For example, when the state raises the minimum wage they will change how and what the employees do so that it seems to work in their advantage. It's much the same when we impose taxes on companies, they just pass that cost off to the customer, and they don't care. On the other hand we can never cut taxes, because I have yet to see the cost of anything deflate because of tax cuts. Tax cuts just mean they make more. It never really trickles down to the people that make the product, at least in any way that can be measured.

The government gives corporation's tax cuts then they in turn match the companies 401K and other programs such as that, because they get a tax cut for them as well. Increasing wages increases their operating expense and therefore affects their bottom line. Investing more money in retirement plans and health care and other programs other than pay, gets them tax deductions rather than expenses. These benefits do provide positive incentives for the employees, but it does nothing to improve their day to day lives. To do that they would have to just pay them more and give more time off, and bonuses for achieving excellent work requirement. I was once told that the fact that we got paid was our bonus for good work; I only wish that the people that gave the bonuses at AIG would see it that way. Meaning: Their pay in the way of bonuses.

The phrase superior supervision is a phase that is supposed to mean that you "do your job." I have already tried to make my case on this subject but I can't help but to try one more time. A team has a leader, the average company has a manager, and a daycare has supervision, the best way to decide what you are doing is to decide what it is that you wish to command. I have worked for leaders that were underpaid, managers that didn't manage, and worst of all I have had supervisors that didn't deserve to command children. I have served with great men: People such as 1stSgt. West, SFC. Irish, SFC, Wolfe, Cpt. Christianson, and so, so many more. These people don't do what they do for money, for fame, or for recognition; they do it because they believe in something.

If I am ever to be remembered as a leader I can only hope that I could be remembered with the likeness of the people that I have mentioned. Much, if not all, of what I am is due to the efforts of people such as them. Example: I was in the field somewhere in Alaska, sleeping in a hole in the ground, and we were on our training phase and they tested our skills routinely. The SgtMaj. approached my hole and asked some question; [it was 25 years ago] and I had no idea what the answer was. I remember being embarrassed not because I looked stupid, but because "Top" was disappointed in me. For the next several months, every time he would see me in the field he would ask me the same question. After I got the question right about a hundred times, he just smiled.

No reprimand, no discipline, just the need for respect of someone that mattered. If companies could operate in this way, and learn to function as a team rather than a company, the glory to be had could truly be celebrated.

The point that I am hinting at in that previous paragraph is that respect is not given, it is earned. If management could learn to act more like a leader and do something to earn that respect, the team would follow. You don't have to be a "Company Man" or "Brown Noser" to do your job. Furthermore, you can't expect your middle or lower management to uphold higher standards and command respect if you don't. That is due to the fact that respect and company attitude comes from the top down.

A good company with good leadership will create good employees, and good products. Set standards and stand by them. Establish a chain of command and stick to it. Create realistic goals and policies, and live by them. It really isn't so difficult, unless you think these things don't apply to you.

Here are some simple criteria for a good leader:

- Only ask someone to do something that you are capable and willing to do.
- Always do more than you expect of others.

- You must be an example to others, and always uphold the standards that you ask of them.
- Communicate what you want, but listen to what they need
- Remember that those who work for you expect you to work for them.
- You have the luxury of never being wrong, so take responsibility when you are.
- Loyalty in the eyes of those who look up to you is the highest rewards you can hope for.
- A leader says follow me, never do it because I told you to.
- Praise costs nothing; to the recipient it is priceless.
- Anyone can tear something down, it take talent to build something up.

Read this list and ask yourself: How many leaders do you know?

Chapter 13

Solutions/Possibilities

*Change does not come, based on the volume of your voice, nor
the volume of voices most heard. Change comes through the
actions and deeds of the few with the courage to stand.
Taxes are used to pay for those things we want, the more we want the higher
the taxes need to be; ask yourself what you would be willing to do without.
The loser is the first to cry foul, when they are beaten, just don't
forget that the only reason they are upset is because they didn't
think of it first. They will do the same thing next time.*

In many of my chapters I have offered several problems and a few solutions. In this chapter I wish to focus on solutions alone. I will probably re-address some issues, but will focus on the potential of positive outcomes. I have always believed that in everything there is the possibility of success, or victory. There simply is no such thing as a war that can't be won, or a goal that is impossible to achieve. Now even though as Steve Martin said, *"it is impossible to fit an elephant up your nose,"* that doesn't mean that, it isn't possible to somehow shrink the elephant, so that it can fit up your nose. I have no idea why we would want to do such a thing, but I think I made my point. I think this is something that is essential and even vital to solving many of the controversies that I have discussed in this book.

Before I dive into the controversies that I mentioned, I would like to address why so dark, and so contentious. I believe that controversy is the best way to have an honest discussion. There are plenty of people that love to discuss the topics of the day with people that all agree with each other. Then again when they discuss things that they may disagree upon then the arguing begins. The interesting thing about controversy is that it is so controversial. However through deep discussion and argument, if you are capable of being human, and nonjudgmental, a person can learn many things. Somebody once said that "the best way to learn is to associate with people that are smarter than you." I must say that I technically disagree because who do the smart people talk to, and how do you judge whether someone is smarter than yourself?

The point of any good discussion isn't to change anyone's minds, or convince people that one opinion is right or wrong. In my opinion the purpose of a good discussion or debate is not to punch holes in those opinions that you oppose, but more importantly discover the holes in your own. We are all capable of figuring out our own opinions, and can develop all the reasoning necessary to truly believe in those facts. I can honestly say that no one has ever changed my mind on any issue just because they said so. I have however changed my mind because new facts came to light, or someone had an argument that caused me to question my beliefs. This may in turn bring new facts to light, resulting in my change of opinion. In my experience there is nobody that I have ever met that changed their minds on a particular subject, just because someone told them they are wrong.

Throughout much of this book I have asserted many of my views on a plethora of subjects. I have stated repeatedly that I only wish to question, and hopefully point out some facts or questions that might make you question. When you question, and think about these types of subjects, whether you agree with me or not, your position on the subject will be strengthened. I have had these types of situation many times, forcing me to go research something for the soul fact that the next time someone argues that point I will be prepared.

I also firmly believe that discussion and debate, as well as a healthy argument, are positive things. When we understand others feelings on a subject it becomes much easier to be tolerant of those opinions. That is what we all really want isn't it? I don't really care if people agree with me, but I would really like to think that people could one day learn to respect the fact that I disagree with them, and there is nothing wrong with that. I have many such examples, and even more that I never even touched on in this book. In many if not all of these examples there are some very simple solutions and some that may be difficult depending on your point of view.

The subject of ethical differences is at times very emotional. As is with many of the subjects that I touched on in that chapter abortion, racism, and capital punishment are but a few. So many of these things would in my opinion simply fade into obscurity if people could just accept that other people are different and have different values. I have yet to have one person ever explain to me how the fact that my wife and I chose to have an abortion years ago affected anyone other than us.

The cold hard fact is that it effects/affects nothing, no one, or anything at all. The best simple solution is to just get over it and yourself. People like Sara Palin and the other morons that think we live in a governmentally controlled state rather than a free one, need to realize that we are not all alike. We live in a complex world or people and opinions. My opinion is that we have a right to choose the path we follow and the lives we live. The only problem I have is with people that wish to dictate. A Dictatorship for right or wrong is the same!

Adolf Hitler: probably the most despised human being on earth, the killer of millions, and the destroyer of nations, ironically developed many of the same ideologies as those who would presume to control all of us. Adolf Hitler supported such things as gun control, he imposed a drinking age and limits on when bars could remain open. The NAZIs further imposed their ideology, by putting warning labels on cigarettes and restricting people from smoking in public places. They controlled what people read and what people were told. They controlled what people could think and do. They did all of this to aid the common person, to help them help themselves, and in building his master race.

If we are to overcome and find those elusive solutions to the controversies that enrage us so: We will need to resist the want or need to control others. I am not talking about anarchy; I am talking about respect.

It is my belief that if we are to drag ourselves out of the Dark Ages, we are going to recognize that our opinions or morals are not the morals of everyone. I believe in Civil Rights, Human Rights, and the Bill of Rights. All of these basically support the understanding that a free people should have these rights.

I believe that if someone wants an abortion, they should have the right to choose to do so. If it is against your values and/or beliefs, then don't. You have that right. Because of the fact that we have freedom of speech, I also believe that anti-abortion activists have a right to protest at clinics, and create advertising to persuade people to not do it. They however do not have the right to deny another person's right to choose.

I would never presume to tell someone that they need have an abortion or that they must own a firearm. So who the hell do you think you are to tell my wife that she should not be able to?

Trying to force another individual to change their beliefs and/or convictions is in my opinion impossible. Laws can be passed, people can be educated, and people will not change their behavior or attitude. A good example of this type of thinking was the passing of XVIII Amendment. (Prohibition 1919-1933) This law was passed as an attempt to impose morality, reduce crime, and make our society more civilized. It cost us billions of dollars, hundreds or thousands of lives, and gave us organized crime. Yet there are still people to this day that will not admit that this law was wrong and did not succeed.

I propose that we address these types of issues differently. In the past we have tried to prevent unwanted pregnancies, by preaching abstinence, made premarital sex a social taboo, and built orphanages all over the country. These are all valid points of view, if you're religious. However we are not all religious and none of these solutions address the root cause of the problem. Sex is a natural act, plain and simple. So if we can't stop people or teens from having sex, we need to address what to do about the pregnancies that will inevitably happen.

The first thing we should do is implement a free program, where women can get counseling, birth control pills, and free medical examinations. Some would say that we already have programs like this. We do! But we don't have laws that truly allow sexually active teens to be protected. I feel that teens should be able to obtain birth control pills, condoms, or any other form of contraceptive with or without parental approvable. There needs to be more sex education in schools. I believe that should include ethical, emotional, and biological education.

People will argue that these types of measures are taking parental rights away. They will argue that these laws will just encourage teens to be more promiscuous. This will lead to more sexually transmitted diseases. It is my opinion that parents have really done nothing to change teen pregnancies in the past. We all know that these kids are and will continue to have sex. Therefore it must be logical that we provide them with the tools and education to make the best choices that they can.

Parents can go on teaching their children about sex and developing their moral values. At the end of the day it is those teens that will ultimately make the decision on whether or not to have sex. Parents cannot be there 24/7!

I have addressed the subject of prevention, now what do we do when that fails? And it will! For the right to life supporters I say this. Bringing a child into the world is a huge financial and legal burden, as well as long term responsibility. If we want people to choose life over abortion, we need to make that choice easier and less burdensome.

I am not talking about increasing welfare for single or underage mothers. For example: We need to transfer financial responsibility to the potential adoptive parents. They pay for the medical bills and all other bills directly related to the child, from the beginning. I also believe that the mothers should be compensated. I also believe that the laws protecting the privacy of the adoptive parents be changed and allow visitation rights.

Lastly we need to stop rewarding single mothers with welfare and earned income credit. I support the philosophy that welfare is a limited short term solution, not a way of life. If a teen gets pregnant, they should be offered five years of welfare. Starting after graduating high school they receive medical treatments and checkups for the child. They receive food stamps, assisted housing supplements and they be awarded a cost of living wage. They would also have the opportunity to go to a community college or state college for free during those five years after graduation. If they fail to graduate, they get no welfare.

If in the case of a single mother over the age of eighteen: The welfare would begin the following day after the child is born. All other requirements are the same. There are no extensions to the five years. Your second or third child is your responsibility. After the five years are up, the mother should have a diploma, and at least some form of college degree, as well as help finding a job. If however after five years the mother is not capable of providing for the child or children, they would at that time become wards of the state and be placed in an adoption agency. Five years is more than enough time to correct a mistake, but at the same time cuts off the people that would try to miss use it. Five is all you get, and you only get it once.

The solutions to our economic problems are more complicated, and will take a lot of work and frankly, faith. Faith not in God, but in doing what is right, not because it is profitable but because it is right. There are many problems to deal with including Health Care, Unemployment, Wall Street, special interest, Global Warming, and Energy Reform. The reality is that these examples only scratch the surface. There have been several books dedicated to each of these subjects and I will try to answer some of these questions as simply as possible.

Maybe the reason all these books that have been written have not solved the problem yet, is because they are so complex and the solutions are harder to understand than the problems. First on the list is the now notorious, Health Care Bill. The controversy and debate was intense and was ongoing as I was writting this. We will probably not hear the end of it for years to come. The problems with the bill are many, but the opinions are even greater. To have a solution to anything one need first to understand what the problems are.

I personally must say that I support the bill. It is interesting in the fact that when I started writing this book, the bill was still in the argument stage, and nobody knew what was going to be in it or if it stood a chance of being law. Of which I mentioned in other parts of the book: the debate was feverish and passionate and anything but "universal", at least in its support. I did believe that it would pass, and right or wrong I am glad it did. This is one of those places where people have the problem.

I am not talking about what their opinions of the bill but rather the fact that it is here. We all know that speeding is against the law yet until you get a ticket it hardly ever enters your mind. This is true with the Health Care Bill as well. I absolutely amazed me when it passed and the talk the next day was about cost and "when did they dream this up?" I actually know educators that I am acquainted with that were unaware of what it was really about. No wonder there are so many misguided and uninformed opinions about it. They were more upset that it was law and they had no say in the matter than they were over what was in the bill, or what was not.

Now I am not going to argue the points of the bill, since I have already made my opinion clear, but I have to address one point. The last two months of endless commercials about how it will kill children and we are going to euthanize grandma, really started to wear on my patience, and nerves. I can honestly say that because of these ridiculous claims, fear tactic rabble rousing, and the endless lies, I will never vote Republican again, and maybe not vote at all. Both parties definitively pissed me off and disappointed me more than I already was.

To put it simply: the problem is that somebody did something and it passed; now we have to deal with it. Some will say that is what scares them the most. How are we going to pay for it? They are going to have to raise taxes. Raising taxes scares people more than they fear God. Compare what that really means for a minute; I am referring to the taxes part.

I will first compare all the financial gains and losses from my personal situation, then from some other average people's point of view, just to try to show a perspective, leading of course to a solution. Prior to losing my job I was making around 35 thousand per year. I paid $170.00 per month or $85.00 per pay check for employer paid health insurance. I know many people that thought that was great because of the cost. I had many friends that paid much more. If you do a little math this is what it looks like from a business point of view.

$35,000.00/26=$1,346.00 per pay period. $85.00 health insurance divided by $1,346.00=6% my wife and I were paying 6% of our income for health coverage before anything else. What else is there? Prescriptions cost at that time $10.00 each for generic and $25.00 for non-generic pills: Then there was my $45.00 "co-pay" for office visits. Strangely enough that is what the office visit cost to begin with. Then there is the magical deduction or $1,000.00 per year and the yearly maximum. With my wife's condition and no children, and not counting me, because I just don't go; our health care breaks down as follows.

	Number of Payments/ Prescriptions	Cost
2 Week Premium	1	85.00
Drugs	10 at $10.00 ea.	100.00
Office visits	1 on average	45.00
Deductable	1000.00/26 pay checks	38.50
		268.50

Then if you average our normal yearly medical bills after deductable./26 Weeks

($5000.00)		192.30
Cost per Paycheck		460.80
Pay per Year	35,000.00	
Weeks	26	
	1,346.15	
Take home pay	1,009.62	

Pay after Health Care	548.82	
Percentage of pay that the Government takes		25%
Percentage of pay that the Hospitals takes		34%

With the figures shown above the government can raise my taxes by 20 percent and I will profit about $4900.00 per year. In fact when I super imposed some simple financial ratios that are normally used for business to make decisions; I found that none of us can afford health care with or without this bill. I would suggest that you run some liquidity and profitability ratios on your own household, and you will see my point. When I ran some solvency ratios on some of my friends, I discovered that if they ran their homes like a business, none of their kids would have health care and they may even have to lay them off or fire them.

During the arguments about health care many people argued that they could afford and liked their coverage. I say if you can truly afford your health coverage you probably don't need it, because you make far too much money. It has always amazed me to think that the people that can afford the insurance are the same people that could probably afford to just pay the bill if they didn't have insurance. According to the national average people pay about $14000.00 per year for health coverage. If you make 100 thousand dollars per year you are already paying 14% health care coverage whether it goes to the government or some doctor. For all of you that would say that it doesn't cost you that much, think again. You may only pay a portion of that, but your employer pays the rest of that. That is money that is calculated as part of your wage. Why do you think that the average wage in the U.S. is $55.00 per hour? If you pay $100.00 per month, your employer would probably pay $300.00 or even more for the rest of the premium. Some estimates put employer contributions as high as 90%.

So even for that person making 100 thousand dollars per year, the government could raise taxes 10% and they would still save money in the long run. Regardless of your opinion, it is law now, and I do not believe that it will be repealed. Reformed and amended yes, but not repealed. The solution is as obvious as the nose on your face. Vote out the politicians that did not support your point of view and continue to support the ones that support your point of view, end of story. As   for the domestic or political terrorist that are breaking windows and making death threats, they should be treated as any other terrorist. I say hunt them down; as my oath stated when I joined the Army: I will defend the Constitution against all enemies foreign and <u>domestic</u>. For those that would argue that the Health Care Bill is against the Constitution, I say the Constitution means whatever the Supreme Court says it means; that is Democracy!

For our seemingly endless supply of other economic problems, when all is said and done the only thing that will really bring back our economy is jobs, and that will take money. People without jobs can't afford to pay their debts, companies that can't collect their debts, lose money and have to lay people off, and the cycle continues. The only real way to fix most of our economic problems as well social issues is to raise taxes. It's just a reality that we are going to have to except at some point.

While I am discussing taxes the aspect of political agenda comes to mind. Fundamentally the Democrats have wanted to raise taxes, in particular on the rich; the Republicans believe that cutting taxes and regulations will solve everything. The problem is that the Democrats want to raise taxes many times for things that won't help anyone. The Republicans are only interested in benefiting the rich so they can stay rich and continue to get richer. This too benefits no one. The Republican Party generally believes that deregulation is the key, even though that same concept is what got us in this mess to begin with. Of course they were all but too happy when the government bailed out the big banks, and auto industry, and they're the same ones against health care. Apparently helping rich people when they are in trouble is acceptable, while helping those who can't help themselves is just wrong.

This is basically the same train of thought on Global Warming. The proponents for Global Warming would raise taxes for all sorts of Green Technology and to hell with everything else. The opponents would say to hell with Green Technology because it's going to cost too much to change. Make no mistake, investing in and changing to environmentally safer technologies are going to cost. What would truly impress me would be if even one of these groups decided to spend some money or effort on preparing for the inevitable. If Global Warming is happening, it is coming and all the Legislation and Green Technology won't change that. It may prevent it from happening again or lesson the effects or duration of the climate change, but it is coming non-the-less. So the solution for Global Warming is to get ready, because once the torpedo is in the water the only thing left to do is calculate the damage.

The solution to the politics of greed and the mistrust of our government is again simple if we can just get people to follow through with their beliefs. As I mentioned with regards to health care, if you truly disagree with this bill vote them out. I predict that is not what will happen as of today; that is not to say that my opinion will not change between now and 2012. History shows that this type of rhetoric doesn't really change anything or anyone's opinions. There were massive protests during Vietnam and the war lasted for twelve years. In the 80's people were convinced that President Reagan was going to doom us all and then won a second term. The same was true for Clinton and Bush Jr. When it comes to politics there are only two solutions: Vote them out or throw them out, through revolt, in either case deal with it and get over it.

Military Solutions are another controversial subject. I have on many occasions heard it said that there is never a good reason for war and there is always a peaceful solution. This is a wonderfully happy way to think, but like many dreams it is just fantasy. I find it hard to believe that anyone would say that we could have stopped Hitler by discussing things and pointing out the error in his thinking. Maybe we could have just asked him nicely to not kill the Jews???

Then people will say "that was different." He was evil, and he was killing innocents and all sorts of other justifications. Yet the war against Saddam Hussein, who did many of the same, things, and did have and use, Weapons of Mass Destruction against his own people, is considered an un-just war. We are talking about a person that murdered his way into office, killed hundreds of thousands of people, committed all manners of civil rights violations, and untold atrocities, and still people call this un-just. Maybe we should have just asked him to stop hurting people. Then again, maybe waiting until he killed million would have been the best thing to do.

People will argue that there are other ways of dealing with these situations. There are always diplomatic sanctions, as well as economic sanctions, such as trade embargos and so forth. The problem is that they don't work. For example let's examine North Korea. Many are not aware that the United States has been at war with North Korea sense

1951. Before anyone points out that the war ended in 53, I would like to explain that all that happened in 1953 was North Korea and The United States signed a cease fire agreement and that agreement has been in place ever since.

The United States as well as many other countries has imposed all sorts of sanctions for decades, and to what end. These sanctions and embargos have done nothing to stop the atrocities committed by the government of North Korea. They haven't stopped them from enlarging their military and have even less effect at deterring them from development nuclear power and weapons. How many have to die, and how long does something like this have to go on before people will think that force is necessary to stop the wrongs that people do.

Using sanctions and other diplomatic methods is like the babysitter telling the kids to be quiet and when they don't, they are more than happy to let you know that they tried. "It's not my fault that they didn't listen." We need to start to ask ourselves, what are we truly willing to do to stop some of these atrocities? In places such as Darfur, Ethiopia, Somalia, and many others we have used sanctions and every other form of peaceful intervention and still these sanctions have done nothing to save the lives of millions. Don't preach to me if you're not willing to do anything about it.

The fact of the matter is we do this every day; at work if you don't do what you're told you can lose your job. Since we can't convince people that driving 55 mph is the right thing to do, we impose penalties and fines, in an effort to force them to comply? The only measure of force that one country has at its disposal to use is military action, which is part of the checks and balances of the global environment. That is the way it has always been, and I am sure that is the way it will always be.

The key to solving any problem or controversy lies in the action taken, not the in-action of talking about it. Learning to respect others and their opinions is imperative to having the ability to compromise. The ability to compromise is what distinguishes us from a dictatorship. I believe that the ultimate compromise is to allow others to live and believe according to their values, and in turn they allow you to do the same.

We can't have freedom of religion if the only religion we allow is other liberal interpretations of our own. When we discuss Islam, most would gravitate toward the Shiite or Sunni beliefs. When the Shia is brought up, it is referred to as extremism or radical, and is not indicative of true Islamic beliefs. The Shia faith or interpretation is just as old as the others and therefore just as valid as the others. It just so happen that the Shiite and Sunni beliefs most resemble our own. We preach tolerance, understanding, and strength through diversity. Then we turn around and try to disallow or demonize all that lies in contrast to our own beliefs. You are more than welcome to be a Muslim as long as you allow women to be equals, you believe in democracy and capitalism.

My point is that we can never achieve what it is we preach if we don't live by those standards ourselves. How can we expect people to respect our rights, when we don't respect theirs? It's similar to when someone tells you that if you stereotype people you are a bigot or racist. By calling you a racist, they are in turn stereotyping you.

Whether we are talking about gun control, religion, free speech, or politics, we must remember that other people have the right to believe differently. If you don't believe that people should own firearms: Don't buy one. At the same time you can't expect everyone to live by your rules.

This is true in the discussion on politics or war. If we are going to cut the budget, then cut the budget. We can't go on believing that we need to cut spending and then assume that it will all come from programs that don't affect what you think is important. We can't go on thinking that we rule the moral high ground and then turn our backs on a repressed people for fear of getting our hands dirty. If an oppressive government was killing its own civilian population for whatever reason we must decide whether we stand on morals and values or do we stand on ideas and rhetoric.

Solutions can at times be hard fought and hard won. Some are not popular and even more will fail, but at the end of the day action is always better than inaction. Allowing a problem to persist because the people involved can't come to an agreement on how to fix it is in my opinion a misuse of power. Metaphorically speaking it would be like letting the house burn down because we can't agree on whether we should go in through the front or back door. In hindsight we can all argue about what we could or should have done different, but right now is when we need to act.

I feel that if we simple start looking at things differently the solutions will come. They may not be perfect solutions, but I was under the impression that the best way to learn is through our mistakes. The mistake of inaction is repeated over and over. In the words of Yoda from Star Wars: *"Do or do not, there is no try."* To try is to fail and to fail is unacceptable. Either our elected officials succeed at making things better or they do not. I say time for new leadership, but I am just one man...

Conclusion

What I Learned

Words to live by: Honesty, Integrity, Loyalty, Courage, and Sacrifice;
all just words, but words that can guide you to the greatest happiness.
If you believe it to be right one should be willing to risk all,
if it is not worth that risk, then it probably isn't right.
To gain knowledge is a great endowment, but it is only what
one does with that knowledge that will ultimately matter.

I decided that in my conclusion I should let you get to know some more things about me as well as what I learned about myself in the process of writing this book. In every endeavor there is something to be learned, and I don't personally think that you can learn something negative. No matter how bad it is there is always a positive aspect that can be derived from even the worst of cases. In this case I have learned many things.

The most important thing that I feel that I learned out of doing this project is the fact that: as my wife put it, I apparently have a lot to say. I was worried to begin with whether or not I would be able to come up with enough material to write a book, I know now that I could have probably rambled on and made it much longer. Even as I write this, I can think of several things that I never touched on. At the same time I feel that I have included enough for you the reader, to be able to, hopefully be encouraged to think, question, and discuss the topics that I have put forward.

A wonderful thing happens when one undertakes an adventure or project that they had never tried before. The first time a person has sex or goes skiing is the best memory of that event that they will probably carry with them forever. No one can replace the feeling you had the first time you drove a car or jumped out of an airplane. I find myself feeling this as I write this book.

I have always enjoyed a challenge, and this has proven to be just that. Writing this has forced me to think deep and hard about some of my convictions and even pushed me to ask a few questions I never thought of. For example, while writing the chapter on solutions, I found that I had no better answers than anyone else. I seriously wish I did have the answers, but I don't. I suppose if it was that simple, we wouldn't have anything to argue about.

It also forced me to research intensely many subjects. While writing the material about history, I unmistakably enjoyed myself. I have been studying, reading, and researching history as long as I can remember. I have also studied under some great Professors such as; Dr. Joe Needham PhD., Dr. John Ernst PhD., Dr. John Stack PhD., and Valarie Gunhus MBA. Needless to say history was not much of a challenge, but some of my personal opinions on things such as economics, politics, science, and even religion, made me think and dig deep. As I have said most of this book is based on my opinions, but I had to search for plausible and reasonable evidence to support some of my theories and conclusions.

For example my chapter on Bigfoot and UFO's are all just my opinions, but I tried to support them with evidence that the average person can find at least stimulating and intriguing. This is also true of the chapter on conspiracies. I find them fascinating and entertaining at the same time yet most are just conjecture.

So the obvious fact that I learned about myself is that I am not very easily convinced, and in my opinion neither should anyone. I have made reference to the need to question many times over the course of this book and I firmly believe that is exactly what we should do. All I ask is; Question our leaders, politicians, doctors, and experts, and question them until they answer the question. Without suppression we should do this and demand that they comply. I have always believed that the only truly stupid question is the one that was failed to ask. So too this is true when it comes to the unbelievable or paranormal. We must remember that just because it isn't in an encyclopedia or accepted as fact, that doesn't mean that it is not real.

I actually started to feel bad about what I had to say about religion, because of the number of people that truly believe in God. I simply was trying to point out my views and how I came to those views, nothing more. Then again I probably offended many people, but that doesn't change my judgment.

There are many subjects in this book; undoubtedly not all are of interest to you. Some may even find their way into the category of ridiculous or stupid. Many times people believe in things that one person or another find silly, I am no different. I tried to include many subjects for the purpose of giving a good overview of what type of person I am. There are many other things that I possibly should have addressed, but maybe I want to keep those for another book.

The authenticity that I wished to bring to the reader is the fact that I will disagree, and if possible, I will explain why I disagree. For those of you that agree I wished to bring you some facts and opinions to support your beliefs. It is always good to feel that you are not alone in your viewpoint or questions. The underlying message is that as people we need not agree on everything, but do need to respect difference of opinion. I realize that in many places I may have offended, but not out of disrespect. There is no need to be polite to be respectful; people are polite to others that they completely disrespect every day, which is just two faced and disingenuous.

I personally believe that honesty is just the best way to respect anyone or anything. Sometimes I may come across as blunt, but I am only saying what I think. There is absolutely nothing to be gained from politeness. I respect those who have enough respect for themselves and me, that they will tell me the truth without dressing it up. There are many things that I disagree with, but I would never try to tell anyone that they should not be allowed to believe whatever it is that they believe.

I happen to be very fortunate in the fact that I have a group of friends that are as diverse as their opinions and theories on the world. At times we can argue like the worst of enemies, and then laugh at each other and crack another beer. There are simply many subjects that we disagree on, and still we are the best of friends. I find it very boring and very uninformative to sit around and discuss things with people I know are going to agree with me. We all have opinions and they deserve to be heard, and respect is the ability to hear those opinions and accept the fact that they don't necessarily agree with you, and in some cases, never will.

I have made a life out of the impossible, and that has served to build my confidence in anything that I decide to do. I was once told that if I dropped out of school that I wouldn't be able to join the Army, or ever get a decent job. Well I did get into the Army without a diploma, and furthermore I went on to have a job in which I made more money than the people that told me I couldn't. When we started the band and decided that we were only going to play the music that we wrote, everyone told use that was impossible. Three albums and over a hundred and twenty copyrights latter, I have to disagree.

Many times I have been discouraged by people that were convinced that I would fail at one thing or another, just to turn around and make them eat their words later. Writing this book is the same; except no one is telling me that I can't do it. This is because I haven't told anyone. I learned that anything is possible if you just do it. If you want to learn to ski, go do it; simple as that. People always have excuses for not doing the things that we want to do. There is the cost, the time, and fear, all of which are excuses, not reasons. The most wonderful feeling that there is: is to snatch victory out of the grip of defeat. To succeed when others are sure you will fail is what drives me every day.

So if I were to choose one most important of all things that I would like to prove to you, I feel it is that you should never live by what others tell you. Live by your heart, do what you will, fight for what you believe, and never back down. If you are compelled to change your mind; do it because it is right, not just because it is popular.

If I had one piece of advice or wisdom to offer, it would be this:

Help all in need.
Mean what you say.
Fight for what you believe.
Play the same way.

Love as if today is the end.
Look to those who do the same.
In the end: no one stands alone.
Remember those, whom before you came

While traversing the implausible or incomprehensible the magnificent
will find the juxtaposition of all that they find superior.

Viva ut Vivus
"Live, that you may live forever"

CPSIA information can be obtained at www.ICGtesting.com
227533LV00001B/31/P

9 781456 760878